STORYTELLING AND OTHER ACTIVITIES FOR CHILDREN IN THERAPY

STORYTELLING AND OTHER ACTIVITIES FOR CHILDREN IN THERAPY

JOHANNA SLIVINSKE
AND LEE SLIVINSKE

WILEY

John Wiley & Sons, Inc.

Library of Congress Cataloging-in-Publication Data:

Slivinske, Johanna, author.
    Storytelling and other activities for children in therapy/Johanna Slivinske and Lee Slivinske.
      p. ; cm.
    Includes bibliographical references and index.
    ISBN 978-0-470-91998-9 (pbk. : alk. paper); ISBN 978-1-118-01529-2 (ebk)
    ISBN 978-1-118-01530-8 (ebk); ISBN 978-1-118-01528-5 (ebk)
    1. Storytelling. 2. Child psychotherapy. 3. Narrative therapy. I. Slivinske, Lee, author. II. Title.
    [DNLM: 1. Psychotherapy—methods. 2. Adolescent. 3. Child. 4. Mental Disorders—therapy. 5. Narration. WS 350.2]
    RJ505.S75S645 2011
    618.92'8914—dc22

                                                    2010049511

Printed in the United States of America

10 9 8 7 6 5 4 3 2 1

*This book is dedicated to our wonderful daughter, Ashley Slivinske,
from whom we have learned so much.*

Contents

Preface

As adults, all of us have memories from childhood, both positive and negative. We all coped with those events as children in our own unique ways, some of us faring better than others. Most of us were able to overcome childhood's challenges and become productive, responsible adults with the ability to contribute toward the betterment of our community and our world. This is the purpose of this book—to provide the tools needed by mental health professionals to assist children in overcoming life's challenges by promoting resilience through storytelling and other activities.

This applied book focuses on providing professionals with the knowledge, insight, and tools needed to support children and their families to improve their lives through the use of storytelling and other activities. It may be used by a variety of professionals in their interactions with children, including therapists, counselors, social workers, psychologists, psychiatrists, play therapists, physicians, nurses, and child welfare specialists, as well as others involved with positive childhood development and resilience. Therefore, usage of this book is applicable in numerous settings such as hospitals, schools, counseling centers, family service agencies, and child welfare organizations, to name a few.

Introductory chapters provide instructions for book usage, guidance regarding storytelling in therapy, and tips for application of the strengths perspective/positive psychology with children, as well as a review of middle childhood development. Information regarding key practice areas with children is included and written in an accessible manner to encourage information sharing with parents and caregivers. Stories and activities for use by children and therapists then follow.

Although the stories in this book are specifically written for those ages 6 to 12, these may also be applicable to other populations with specific needs, such as adolescents or adults who are dealing with unresolved issues arising in childhood. Stories may be modified appropriately to address the needs of these groups, if desired. Utilization of the book as a textbook for students aspiring to become professionals is another way in which this book may be of benefit in the university environment.

The origin of this book had its roots in both our personal and professional lives, where we have witnessed far too many children experiencing difficulty coping with both the positive and negative aspects of life. Our hope was to provide an additional way by which therapists could enable children to express their emotions surrounding challenging life events in a safe environment with a trusted mental health professional, and to discover their inner strengths to promote resilience for life. Many relevant challenges of childhood, as well as strengths, are explored.

This practical, easy-to-use applied book for therapists' use with children between the ages of 6 and 12 provides a wide range of topical, reality-based stories, story starters, and related activities pertinent to therapy with children, in addition to brief reviews of salient key practice issues. The relevant issues covered in this book include: illness and disability, school issues, anger and behavioral issues, social adjustment and shyness, divorce and parental separations, domestic violence, community violence, trauma and child abuse, substance abuse, cultural and religious issues, fun/happiness and strengths, accidents and injuries, job loss and poverty, military and international violence issues, and death. Many children will identify with these life challenges and will require assistance in overcoming them.

Activities may be freely reproduced from the associated website, making them readily accessible to the therapist and the child. The accompanying website may be used to print stories and worksheets for their sessions. It also permits therapists to individualize, customize, and personalize stories and questions to more closely meet their needs and those of children and their families. When used as a textbook, educators may also personalize activities for classroom role-play activities.

Less specific activities are provided, which also may be used for a wide variety of practice areas with children. Photographs may be used therapeutically by encouraging children to free-write about topics relevant to their therapy goals. Additionally, salient practice suggestions for mental health practitioners are included for each practice area. Many of these suggestions are suitable for sharing with parents, grandparents, guardians, and other family members of children in therapy.

As an aid to the therapeutic process, the activity sheets relevant to each story have been assigned four levels of inquiry representing readiness for self-disclosure. Level 1 questions are designed to be the least threatening and require a minimal amount of self-disclosure and insight. Levels 2 and 3 story questions, respectively, require progressively more self-disclosure and insight, while the Level 4 activity sheet culminates in the highest level of intensity and disclosure. Here, the child, if ready, directly confronts the presenting situation. Using the various levels of inquiry allows children to express their emotions, feelings, and beliefs with a trusted mental health professional at their various levels of readiness.

We sincerely hope that *Storytelling and Other Activities for Children in Therapy* assists you in performing your inherently challenging and important work. You are easing the pain of children who are hurting, and that is truly invaluable. By helping children surmount life's obstacles and discover their innate abilities and strengths, you are helping us all.

Johanna D. Slivinske, MSW

Lee R. Slivinske, PhD

Acknowledgments

We would like to extend our sincerest thanks to all of our friends and family, who have supported us throughout the writing process and who have taught us numerous valuable life lessons. We would like to dedicate this book to our lovely daughter, Ashley Slivinske, and recognize her suggestions for and contributions to the book, including writing the story "Seeing My Friend in a Wheelchair." Thank you also for your understanding while we were writing, for providing encouragement, and for reminding us of what it means to be a child.

We are especially grateful to the many colleagues at Youngstown State University who have supported our endeavor, offered assistance, and guided us while writing this heartfelt therapy book for children. We would like to extend special recognition for our consultations with the following committed colleagues: Dr. Joseph L. Mosca, reviewer, Mr. Vincent Stigliano, reviewer, Mr. Joseph Mistovich, and Dr. Michael J. Murphy. Mr. Carl Leet deserves special thanks and acknowledgment for his contributions of emotion-provoking photographs. Additionally, we would like to thank the Bitonte College of Health and Human Services and our students and clients, who taught us so much over the years.

Thanks are extended as well to John Wiley & Sons, notably to our talented editors, Isabel Pratt and Rachel Livsey; dedicated editorial assistant, Kara Borbely; diligent production editor, Leigh Camp; and vice president and publisher, Peggy Alexander for their guidance and support on this meaningful project. We also appreciate all of the behind-the-scenes efforts contributed by the entire Wiley team and the invaluable suggestions and comments from all of the reviewers. We value your professionalism and graciousness.

In memoriam, we would like to recognize our friend, Lisa Hamrock Mumford; Lee's sister, Gae Roach; and our parents, Donald J. and Frances Detwiler, and

W. LeRoy and Aline Slivinske, for molding us into the people we are today. Thank you for providing so much joy, compassion, and understanding in all of our lives. We continue to learn from and be inspired by all of you yet today.

Johanna D. Slivinske, MSW

Lee R. Slivinske, PhD

Foreword

When my good friend Johanna (whom I have known since middle school) asked that I write the foreword to her book *Storytelling and Other Activities for Children in Therapy*, I of course was honored, but then wondered how someone with a PhD in microbiology and immunology was qualified to write on the topic of storytelling for children in therapy. I am not an expert in the field of social work or child psychology. I am a parent, which on a good day qualifies me as somewhat of an expert on children (or at least an expert on my three boys). I was once long ago a child myself.

It was as I began to read *Storytelling* that I realized why I could write the foreword to this book. I could look back to my childhood and relate to so many of the stories and the scenarios described. "My Mom" (in chapter 5) was especially pertinent, as my own mother was diagnosed with cancer when I was only 5 years old. Over the next 20 years she battled the disease in one way or another, and the older I got, the more I understood, and the worse I would feel. My family has always been close, but there was the mentality of "pulling yourself up by your bootstraps," which was not always compatible with allowing one to discuss feelings or even admit needing help. I also thought I wasn't the one who was sick, so just what did I have to worry/complain/cry about? I know my parents tried their best to be there during these difficult times (including my mother), but there comes a time, for whatever reason, when parents, relatives, and friends cannot provide the support a child might need, no matter how hard they try. I can only wonder at times if someone had presented this story to me and had asked me how I felt about my mom having cancer, would I have been better able to deal with it? Would I have been more willing to talk and to express my feelings?

As a mother, I hope that I will be able to provide the emotional support that my children need growing up in today's society. My husband and I have tried to raise our children in a home where open and frank discussions are welcome and in an environment where they can express themselves. However, if there ever comes a time when I feel we are not providing the emotional support they need, then we will encourage them, and help them, to find the resources they need, whether that be in the form of activities such as drawing or sports or as therapy.

I believe Johanna and Lee Slivinske have penned a book full of stories using pertinent topics in today's society in which to help children explore their feelings on a wide range of topics, from witnessing parents' divorce to the deaths of friends/relatives to exploring a child's inner strengths and gifts. This book is a valuable resource to social workers and parents alike, as a springboard for discussing life-changing events in a society that is too busy to listen.

Hester Doyle, PhD
Yale University, New Haven, CT

CHAPTER 1

How to Use This Book

This is not the type of book that must be read from cover to cover. It may be opened to the practice area and story or activity that is most pertinent to the needs of the children you are counseling. Each chapter briefly discusses salient, key practice areas and relevant issues about therapeutic topics. The key practice areas are written in an accessible manner to encourage sharing of relevant information with parents and caregivers of children. Story selection is then discussed and recommendations for use provided.

The therapeutic stories and activities follow, and are designed for use by children approximately between the ages of 6 and 12 years, with the assistance and guidance of a professional. Although the stories are specifically written for children in middle childhood, these may also be applicable to other populations with specific needs, such as adolescents or adults dealing with unresolved issues arising in childhood. Stories may be modified appropriately to address the needs of these groups, if desired.

The introductory chapters in this applied book may be used by practitioners to learn customization of activities, to enhance their knowledge base and application of storytelling techniques in therapy with children, and to expand their knowledge of strengths-based practice and positive psychology. In addition, a section is included to refresh practitioners' memories regarding childhood developmental issues. These chapters may be read, referred to when needed, and serve as available reference material for practitioners.

Storytelling is the primary vehicle to be used in this book. As professionals are aware, counseling children involves both art and science (Webb, 1991). The therapists using this book should be professionally educated in their respective fields and should draw upon their own training, knowledge base, and theoretical philosophy and apply this toward working with children.

Consider the five following points of distinction when counseling children in general, which also may apply when utilizing techniques of therapeutic storytelling. These will help practitioners to build rapport and trust in the therapeutic alliance as well as promote coping, problem solving, and healthy skills for life. The five "E's" of therapy with children follow:

> *Engage.* Appeal to the child's sense of curiosity and catch the child's interest. Use props, toys, and games when appropriate and encourage the child to relax and to open up. Increase the child's comfort level by making the playroom or office child-friendly, yet not overly stimulating.

> *Entertain.* Although therapy may at times be "hard work," there is no reason therapists cannot "entertain" a child in treatment. At times, use toys or games that the child likes, not always necessarily what the practitioner likes. If a child feels particularly stressed by an activity or story, take a break and return to it later. Find an activity to relieve stress, perhaps a video game, to briefly give the child a mental break. When appropriate, laugh and joke with the child. It is OK for the child and the therapist to smile and laugh.

> *Emote.* Freely support children to openly express their emotions in a comfortable, protective setting instead of suppressing them. These emotions include feeling angry, sad, confused, and the like, as well as feelings of joy and happiness. Expressing sad or angry emotions may serve as a healthy emotional release in a positive, supportive environment. How to cope with these intense emotions in healthy ways may then be taught. Happy feelings may serve as stress relief in therapy and in life. Happiness and joy contribute to resilience building.

> *Educate.* Much of what therapists do is teach, and children want and need to learn. Therapists teach coping skills, social skills, problem-solving techniques, life skills, and so forth. Utilize the stories and activities in this book as opportunities for teachable moments in the lives of children.

> *Encourage.* Encourage children to do their best, and believe in them and their ability to achieve and overcome adversity. Mental health professionals may also serve as coaches and cheerleaders for children with whom they are working. One person can make a difference in their lives. Build upon the innate assets, gifts, competencies, and strengths that individual children possess, and encourage them to further develop their unique talents and gifts.

Specifically regarding this book, this collection of stories is designed to assist children in exploring a wide range of thoughts, emotions, and life issues. The activities in this book are designed to be practical, easy to understand, and user-friendly. Meaningful therapeutic interaction can be achieved as children answer thought-provoking questions and write about, talk about, or draw their own endings to stories. Role-playing, music, and acting also may be used at the discretion of individual therapists (see chapter 20, General Activity Sheets for All Practice Areas, for suggestions). These may be done in-session with aid from a therapist, or the exercises may be completed as homework assignments when appropriate. Discussion of the stories in a therapeutic setting with a mental health professional can lead to enhanced assessment and treatment of children and preteens.

Stand-alone activities are also provided. Quizzes, questionnaires, sentence completions, drawing activities, acrostic poems, the CHILD mind-set tool pages, and the like provide valuable insight and information regarding the child's emotional state and life circumstances. Certain photographs in this book may be used to relax therapists between sessions and may serve a therapeutic purpose by having the child free-write or draw about how the picture makes him or her feel by eliciting emotional responses relevant to the child's treatment goals.

Additionally, many of the stories in this book may help build the therapeutic relationship with the child. Other, more emotionally challenging stories or activities may be more appropriate to use with children once there is a strong therapeutic relationship already in existence. This way, a trusting, healing environment exists for the child to feel comfortable and shielded from danger, real or imaginary. Here, the child can rely on the practitioner to support and comfort him or her emotionally. Therefore, the practitioner must determine each child's readiness to delve into highly charged emotional matters (Crenshaw, 2008).

The therapist also should monitor the emotional response of the child to ensure that the child is capable of emotionally handling the information. If the therapist helps to rewrite the story with the child, he or she may decide to add features that include themes of protection and safety. The therapist also should try to regroup prior to ending the session, ensuring the child is feeling safe and protected (Lieberman & Van Horn, 2008).

Activities have been specifically designed for use with each individual story and problem area. Specific questions accompany each story. The activity sheets may be used as is or modified to use with other stories and key practice areas at the discretion of the practitioner.

The activity questions have been written in a manner to encourage self-disclosure and to facilitate dialogue between the practitioner and the child. Four levels have been assigned to activity sheets dependent on given expectations of the child and the practitioner. Readiness for self-disclosure, ability to handle emotional confrontation, strengths of the therapeutic relationship, support in the home environment, timing, pacing, and developmental appropriateness must all be considered when deciding how to assign activity sheets to any given child client.

The story activity sheets have been labeled to indicate progression of self-disclosure on the part of the child. These activity sheets have been assigned labels of Levels 1, 2, 3, and 4, respectively. Suggestions regarding how to choose the level needed for specific clients are given below.

Level 1 story activity questions are designed to be the least threatening for the child. These are written about other people, children, and life situations. These require the least amount of self-disclosure and insight into self. The child may respond to questions pertinent to the specific story and then create an ending to that particular story. He or she may identify with characters in the story and may or may not choose to divulge information or similarities regarding his or her own life circumstances and emotions. The practitioner must decide when it is appropriate to advance to the next level.

Level 2 story activity questions require slightly more disclosure on the part of the child. He or she is asked questions pertinent to the topic area discussed in the story. However, the questions are directed toward others that the child may know or know of. Questions are posited regarding whether the child knows of someone who has had problems or life situations similar to the characters in the story. The child may then write an ending to a story for this "friend" or "person" (real or imaginary) that he or she knows of. The child may also rewrite or change some aspect of the story, building in an element of control. This enables the child to discuss emotionally challenging material through a less threatening medium than directly addressing issues within himself or herself. If desired, the more generic General Story Activity Sheet (see chapter 20) may be substituted for the Level 2 story activity sheet if a less specific, less threatening activity is more relevant for a specific child in a particular circumstance.

Level 3 involves a higher level of disclosure, where the child is asked questions pertinent to the topic area discussed. Now, however, the questions are directed toward situations in the child's life. He or she may be asked whether life situations similar to those of story characters have happened to the child or someone close to him or her, such as a family member. This may be more intense for some children, especially those who are socially inhibited or shy. The child may then write an ending to a story for himself, herself, or a close family member. The child may also rewrite or change some aspect of the story, building in an element of control. Not all children will be ready to disclose at this level, while others may welcome the chance to discuss their life situations.

Level 4 also involves a higher level of intensity and disclosure and asks the child to directly write his or her own story, beginning to end, usually about his or her own life. It allows for a high level of creativity on the part of the child as well as for freewriting or drawing on a blank page. The practitioner may provide as much or as little guidance or instruction as desired to achieve the child client's individualized treatment goals. This same activity sheet may be used to enable the child to write or draw any type of story relevant to his or her particular needs, not necessarily at a higher level of intensity or disclosure. It may also be used as a space to write or draw stories to accompany Activity Levels 1, 2, and 3.

Again, practitioners must exercise professional judgment when deciding which stories, activities, and activity levels are suitable for any given child. At times, levels may be modified or skipped when appropriate. Various treatment modalities may be employed, including storytelling, writing, drawing, drama, and others.

When using this book with various populations, therapists must use their own professional training and discretion when determining which stories to use with particular clients. According to Frantz (1995), a story should be pertinent to the needs of the listener or reader. The practitioner must decide which stories are relevant to the specific needs of their clients.

Also, these stories were designed with specific problems, challenges, or situations in mind (see Contents). Although they were designed for special situations, they were also written in such a way to allow for clients to "make them their own." At times, details were purposely left out to enable children to finish the stories with their own details. Vagueness can be positive in therapeutic storytelling and may allow for clients "to step into the story" (Frantz, 1995, p. 55).

Customization of Activities

While all of the included activities are ready to use in the therapeutic setting in their current state, some practitioners may want to customize or personalize the activities for particular children. This may elicit a more positive response from a particular child. Simple ways to customize include the following:

➤ Problems or strengths in the stories could be more closely tailored to the child's situation.

➤ Names of characters may be changed to allow for closer cultural identification with the characters.

➤ Gender of the characters could also be changed to allow for closer identification with the characters.

Customization of activities may be pertinent to use with children who are ready to move from indirectly writing or talking about story characters to more directly telling their own story. Samples of ways to personalize the activities include:

➤ Placing the child's name on the activity sheet or in the story

➤ Placing a photograph of the child on the story page where appropriate

➤ Adding specific personal details about the child such as hair color, eye color, glasses, and so on

➤ Adding details about events and places in the child's life such as birthdays and schools attended

➤ Adding names of friends, family members, teachers, and pets

➤ Adding activities that a child participates in such as soccer, baseball, band, scouts, and so forth

Example of Customization of Stories

Scenario 1

Keisha is an 8-year-old African American girl being raised by her single mother, Janice. Janice is a member of the Air Force Reserve, who was called to active duty and deployed to serve in Afghanistan. Keisha now is living with her maternal grandparents, Mr. and Mrs. Wallace. Keisha is struggling to adapt to her mother's deployment and her new living arrangements with loving grandparents.

When customizing stories, the practitioners may modify the characters' gender, name, family situations, and environmental factors to meet the needs of their child clients. The following story has been customized to better apply to Keisha's life situation.

Original "My Dad" Story

Hi, my name is Devon. I don't understand why Dad had to leave. He has been away before, but this time is different. He is in a war on the other side of the world. I miss him so much and I am really afraid. I don't want anything bad to happen to him.

I just want him to come home and so does my mom. We have all been working extra hard while he is away. We have so many extra chores now. Mom even has to cut the grass. Sometimes she cries while she watches the news. I just want everything to go back to normal.

Sample Customization of "My Dad" Story

Hi, my name is Tanika. I don't understand why Mom had to leave. She has been away before, but this time is different. She is in Afghanistan. I miss her so much and am really afraid. I don't want anything bad to happen to her.

I just want her to come home and so do my grandparents. Grandma and Grandpa are nice, but they are just not my mom. Sometimes Grandma cries when she watches the news. I just want everything to go back to normal.

When the child client is ready for further disclosure about herself, the "My Story" activity sheet could be customized in the following way, allowing the child to elaborate on her own story with help from her therapist:

Hi, my name is Keisha, and this is my story. My mom is a soldier and got sent to Afghanistan. Now I live with my grandparents. I love my grandparents, but I miss my mom.

The child could then be instructed, if ready emotionally, to complete her own story. When customizing stories, the therapist could assist in the storytelling process if desired and when appropriate. This fosters an interactive quality in the storytelling process. Customization may allow for an opportunity for increased self-expression and articulation of feelings on the part of the child. It also may promote facilitation of specific functional outcomes delineated by individual therapists.

When assisting in the storytelling process, practitioners will sometimes strive to achieve positive outcomes from the characters. The therapist may assist the child in constructing ways in which characters may take appropriate and healthy steps toward achieving real-life goals and plans (Burns, 2005). This may empower the child to further develop desirable methods of dealing with challenges in his or her own life.

Because the stories in this book are mainly reality based, if the child does write a story ending with a negative ending or outcome, it may be a positive and healthy means of expressing emotions that may otherwise be suppressed. Once the practitioner feels this has occurred and the emotions effectively processed, he or she must decide whether to proceed with the child in rewriting the ending or outcome to the story. This is partially based on the individual circumstances of the child's life situation, emotional readiness, developmental appropriateness, timing, and the strength of the therapeutic relationship.

If the decision is made to rewrite a negative story ending with an alternate ending, the story may then be reconstructed to include constructive steps that need to be taken in order to facilitate change in the characters' lives, and consequently, the child's life. Development of effective problem solving and coping skills can be achieved in this manner (Burns, 2005). However, always consider the specific situational details of each child's life.

In general, try to match the story with the unique experiences of the child. Also, modify stories when appropriate by altering the character's problem/strength or role to meet the needs of the child. Additionally, identify and address the child's individualized developmental, situational, and salient needs and strengths. This will assist in further reaching the child and in enhancing the strength of the therapeutic relationship.

Situations in Which This Book Can Be Used

This storytelling method may assist children who have difficulty expressing their emotions directly (R. A. Gardner, 1971). Also, respecting the individual needs of each unique child, his or her circumstances, and goals of treatment is essential (Webb, 1991). Using this book, therapeutic information may be gained regarding various topics, including:

> ➤ Illness and disability
> ➤ The home/school environment (including bullying and learning disabilities)
> ➤ Emotional and behavioral challenges
> ➤ Social competence and shyness
> ➤ Divorce and separation

- ➤ Domestic violence
- ➤ Community violence
- ➤ Trauma and child abuse
- ➤ Familial substance abuse
- ➤ Cultural issues
- ➤ Happiness and strengths
- ➤ Accidents and injuries
- ➤ Parental job loss and poverty
- ➤ Military issues and international violence
- ➤ Death

At the discretion of the practitioner, stories and activities also may be applied to topics not mentioned above. Through analysis and discussion of children's written, verbal, or drawn endings to stories, effective problem-solving techniques also may be learned. Emotions may be expressed in a nurturing environment, with comforting emotional support given by therapists and family members. Extremely important coping mechanisms may be fostered and incorporated into children's lives. Significant treatment issues may be addressed from the perspective of the child at his or her current level of developmental readiness.

One storytelling method that may be utilized in a therapeutic manner when using the activities in this applied book is called the "Progressive Story" (Divinyi, 1995). This method is particularly useful when working with populations who have limited introspection and problems with self-disclosure. In the progressive story, the clinician or group facilitator begins the story, and the client or group writes and finishes the story (Divinyi).

This method has been used successfully with groups of adolescent girls placed in residential facilities. For example, a group of girls met weekly and created the story of a girl's life. Much was gained through this therapeutic technique. The group leader would ask questions such as "What is she thinking?" or "How is she feeling?" (Divinyi, 1995, p. 33). This evoked emotional reactions and expressions of feeling from the girls. Although they were unable to directly express emotions about themselves, they were able to identify with the character in the story, which allowed them to express their emotions through her (Divinyi).

The progressive storytelling technique also allows children to plan future behavior of the characters. By planning for the future and making difficult decisions about the lives of characters, clients can see the benefits of positive decisions that characters make versus those decisions that could adversely impact the characters' (and their own) lives. For example, in the previously mentioned group of girls, a girl had suggested "Why don't we have her kill her father?" (Divinyi, 1995, p. 33). In the group process, group members decided that this would result in a negative outcome.

This, however, did allow the girls to vent their feelings of anger, regarding child abuse by parents, in a safe environment (Divinyi).

The progressive storytelling technique has value for all populations, including children. Application of the method has validity for use with individuals and groups as a supplemental technique in addition to the practitioner's own theoretical orientation and knowledge base. Also, it can be modified to suit the needs of both therapists and children. This technique is beneficial in assisting therapists to improve the quality of lives of those they serve.

2

Principles and Processes
of Therapeutic Storytelling

Therapeutic storytelling is a technique that is beneficial in guiding practice for children from preschool age through adolescence. It may be used as a technique with individual children and also may be used with their parents or caregivers in a family therapy setting. Therapy may be directed through story selection that is tailored for specific issues, such as death, domestic violence, or child abuse, to name a few. Healing can occur as children learn from and identify with characters in stories, which may enable them to recover from traumatic experiences. During this process, practitioners can point out similarities between characters and children's lives to help them explore their own life experiences and situations (Geldard & Geldard, 2008).

Children may discover facets of stories that encourage them to look toward and develop plans for their own futures. Certain stories will reach and meet the needs of some individuals more than others. Often, a story is much more than it appears on the surface. Relevant stories benefit children by offering hope, instilling values, promoting optimism, and creating a sense of not being alone in a situation. Stories may remove children from themselves, yet empower transformation of themselves (Livio, 1994).

Mental health professionals should exercise their best judgment as to readiness of the child to move from indirect, less threatening, displaced story material to directly addressing and applying information to a child's actual reality-based problem or situation (Webb, 1991). Deciding when and how to do this is based partially on the art of working with children, with careful consideration of a child's emotional state, strength of the therapeutic relationship, and timing. Children need to know they are cared for by adults in their lives, including their therapists. Offering caring support and comfort may facilitate self-expression from the child.

Narrative therapy as a means of practice with families is now included as an important component of many psychotherapy and family therapy manuals and textbooks (Angus & McLeod, 2004; Carr, 2007; Nichols, 2008). Storytelling is widely recognized as an integral element of narrative therapy. In addition, many cultures have a strong, rich oral tradition of transmitting family and cultural stories to younger generations. Storytelling in general has been shown to have a positive impact on people's mental health (Gardner & Poole, 2009). When applied to children in therapy, storytelling can help clients to more fully understand and change their own complex situations.

Storytelling comes naturally to many children and is an effective way for them to divulge what they are thinking and feeling. It also opens a door to plan for events and provides them with hope for the future. Stories may be built in conjunction with the therapist, and may be constructed around life experiences with friends and family members. A positive approach to storytelling may also be incorporated, which entails focusing on strengths and assets identified in their lives and stories (Helton & Smith, 2004).

Additionally, each practitioner needs to determine the developmental appropriateness of each story for each particular client. The stories should be modified by the practitioner if they are above or below the appropriate developmental level. Language also may be adjusted to allow for easier understanding or processing of the story. This also applies in situations where children have developmental disabilities or limitations that would require story adjustments.

The utilization of a technique called "lifemapping" has shown to benefit those with learning disabilities when articulating their life narratives, or stories of their lives. Lifemapping involves the process of drawing and writing the story of one's life by inserting words, dates, drawings, and emotions surrounding important life events into circles or shapes connected by lines or arrows on a sheet of paper. These visually represent the story of one's life from the time of birth to the present. These are subjective and individualized to each person's unique circumstances (Gray & Ridden, 1999). For an example, refer to the "Lifemap" activity sheet included in chapter 20. Lifemaps may also assist in expression of life events and emotions for children who have experienced multiple relocations or traumas in their young lives.

If a traumatic event has occurred, experiencing the trauma again through reading, interpreting, and retelling of stories allows the child to reprocess the traumatic event in a protective setting, which aids in resolving issues and emotions surrounding the trauma. Healing can occur as children learn and identify with characters in stories that enable them to recover from traumatic experiences (Golding, 2006). At first, it may be beneficial to discuss the feelings and events of the characters in the story, instead of directly addressing the child's situation or problem. Using this indirect approach with children may be less threatening than immediately and directly addressing their life situation or trauma (Golding). The therapist must decide when and if to advance toward more direct confrontation of the child's unique circumstances based on emotional readiness, pacing, state of the therapeutic alliance, and treatment goals.

When children hear stories, they often identify with the characters and events in the stories. This helps them reflect on their own experiences, which may be similar to the experiences and emotions of the characters. Processing, gaining understanding, and finding resolution of their own emotional issues may then occur. Hopefully, they also may learn that it is beneficial to share and experience powerful emotions in a supportive and caring environment (Geldard & Geldard, 2008; Golding, 2006).

When children make connections between stories and their own lives, they may then be capable of exploring their own life experiences. When creating their own stories, children are likely to include ideas about their own real-life experiences. They may make themselves characters or expound on their own life events. Thoughts, experiences, feelings, and actions may be indirectly or directly explored (Geldard & Geldard, 2008). At times, the stories may be told and retold, with the child's problems no longer being prominent. Deconstruction and reconstruction of the stories may be helpful (Morgan, 2000). By finishing stories in a positive manner, children may find hope that their life situations can also improve (Golding, 2006). For example, if the child writes or tells negative or dysfunctional endings to a story, the therapist should explore what this means to the particular child and examine the events and emotions surrounding the story. The child, the therapist, or both can then "rewrite" or "retell" the story in a more positive manner with a more positive outcome, if desired. Future positive life goals and possibilities may also be explored.

Stories also may make children feel less alone in the world. This may be especially true in instances of child abuse, substance abuse, or domestic violence. In these instances, children are likely to believe that they are the only ones that suffer from these particular problems. They may be relieved to find that other people experience the same issues. This may allow them to divulge or share more information about their own situations (Geldard & Geldard, 2008). It may also help children gain valuable understanding of their life situations and to find comfort and empathy in knowing they are not isolated or alone (Golding, 2006). Telling their own stories about their traumatic experiences can be an important component in the healing process for children (Cohen, Mannarino, & Deblinger, 2006).

Books and stories may also be used to educate children regarding appropriate behaviors. These may be utilized to address various issues such as "abuse, violence, social skills, anger management, sex education, separation, divorce and death" (Geldard & Geldard, 2008, p. 214). Examination of many of these important issues occurs in various stories and activities throughout this book.

Additional tips for using storytelling as a therapeutic technique include the following:

➤ Model how to create a story if this helps the child.

➤ Make it as fun as possible for the child.

➤ Allow the child to say the story aloud if he or she prefers, while the therapist writes down the story (Geldard & Geldard, 2008).

➤ Match the feelings and events conveyed in the story with the needs of the child (Golding, 2006).

➤ Do not force the child to read or complete a story if he or she is not ready to do so (Golding, 2006).

➤ Record the child's voice or video record the child telling the story and play it back for the child.

➤ Allow the child alternative means of expressing his or her story, such as through painting, drawing, singing, dancing, or acting.

➤ Use props such as puppets or dolls for younger children to assist in telling their stories.

➤ Enable the child to use a microphone, or walkie-talkies as part of the play therapy experience when telling stories.

➤ Allow the child to "text," "email," or "video mail" stories in the context of play therapy.

➤ Be patient and allow time for the child to be comfortable with the story.

➤ Allow expression of creativity for both the child and the therapist.

➤ Therapists should not be afraid to use this method if they feel they are not proficient storytellers (Divinyi, 1995).

Interpretive Aspects of Children's Storytelling Artwork

Encouraging artistic expression in the therapy setting benefits individuals who may have difficulty interacting with others verbally and for whom emotional expression is threatening. Those who are unable to communicate in a conventional manner, such as those experiencing hearing impairments, may find an alternative means of expression through this medium. In addition, therapeutic use of art creates a tangible means of expression allowing for a nonverbal comfort zone between the therapist and child (Josephs, 2005).

Emotions, feelings, and ideas can be conveyed through the artwork and drawings of children. Remember that artistic ability is partially dependent on the age and developmental level of the child producing the art. If drawing is to be used in this book, it does not need to be used in a diagnostic manner per se, as interpreting artwork is an extremely subjective process. However, the basic emotions expressed through their artwork may be able to be identified. They may express being happy, sad, mad, or afraid through their drawings. Dialogue between the child and therapist about the artwork is most important here. If the emotion can be identified, it may be used to understand its origin and pertinent issues surrounding the emotion.

Children's emotional states are often expressed within their drawings and paintings. This may increase their feelings of freedom and allow them to express emotions in an individualized manner. Some children may experience increased comfort levels if their therapist and other loved ones also draw or paint a picture (Helton & Smith, 2004). Bear in mind that children's artwork expresses inner reflections of emotions and insights into their internal world (Clements, Benasutti, & Henry, 2001).

In general, children express their emotions in three basic ways through art: (1) literally, (2) through content, and (3) through abstraction. When an emotion is expressed literally, a human face will often be shown expressing a smile or a frown. Younger children will simply show a simple curved line to show either a happy or sad face. Literal expression is also more common among younger children. Literal expression involves personification of animals or objects such as trees and flowers. For example, a tree may be shown smiling (Jolley, 2010).

Content drawings often depict real-life events and moods. For example, a gray, rainy, dreary outdoor day may depict sadness. A bright sunshiny day with children swinging on a backyard swingset may depict happiness (Jolley, 2010). It may also represent recent events in the child's life.

Artwork that lacks content and is composed of various lines or shapes may be considered abstract. Bright colors may be representative of a happier mood of a child (Jolley, 2010). Keep in mind, however, that all artwork is open to subjective interpretation and is to be used as only one tool when helping a child. Different professionals with different training may interpret the artwork in a unique manner. However, it is a very useful technique in allowing the child to express his or her emotions in a positive and safe way.

Culture also influences the artwork of children. One interesting finding involving drawings of children is that the genitalia of people are usually not drawn by children in Western cultures, unless there has been some type of sexual abuse or observation of sexuality. This differs vastly from the drawings of children in areas of Africa and Asia where clothing is not always worn. In these areas, it is much more common for the genitals and breasts to be drawn by children who are developing typically and who have not been abused and do not have any negative emotional issues (Paget, 1932, as cited in Jolley, 2010).

Thus, be mindful of cultural influences when interpreting all drawings and artwork of children. Also, mindfulness of changes in our own society, notably the availability of sexual material via the Internet and television, may contribute to children's premature exposure to sexually graphic material. Exposure to such material has the potential to influence children's artwork.

Overview of Additional Therapy Techniques

Discussion of the stories in a therapeutic environment with a mental health professional can lead to enhanced assessment and treatment of children and preteens. Elements of bibliotherapy, play therapy, art therapy, control theory, and the strengths perspective can also be utilized and/or combined with storytelling. This section provides a brief overview of the aforementioned therapy techniques.

In general, bibliotherapy involves using written material such as books, poetry, or literature to assist in the therapeutic process. It has been shown to be effective when used with groups and individuals (Barker, 2003). By encouraging children to express their emotions and ideas about their life situations, achievement of therapeutic gains may occur. Valuable skills such as coping may be taught through reading and discussion (DeLucia-Waack, 2006). In this book, bibliotherapy techniques have been adapted to use with children between the ages of 6 and 12. Very short stories are included that will hold and capture the young reader's attention. Specifically written to address particular real-life situations, challenges, and strengths, these stories and activities assist in empathic, reality-based problem resolution as well as planning for a positive future.

Play therapy is a particular type of therapy often employed by play therapists, social workers, counselors, psychologists, nurses, and other professionals. It has been found to be helpful in engaging and opening lines of communication with children and sometimes even adults. In this regard, toys and games are used to assist children in expressing emotions, demonstrating conflicts, and solving problems, which they may be unable to communicate verbally (Barker, 2003; Webb, 1991). Play is an essential component of human development. Through therapeutic play, building of coping skills may occur (Josephs, 2005).

Most children enjoy playing games, and these tend to be particularly effective for use in the group setting. Traditional games may be modified to facilitate communication and to teach problem-solving techniques. Adaptation of familiar games such as tag, hot potato, musical chairs, or hide-and-seek may improve friendship-building abilities and teamwork (Carlson, 1999). Nontherapeutic games may also be utilized to assess a child's social interaction abilities and frustration tolerance, and as a reward when played at the end of a session (Schmidt, 2001). Play therapy techniques may be combined with storytelling to enhance treatment. For example, using puppets and dolls to tell stories will improve therapeutic communication for some children. Creation of games specific to particular stories serves as a complementary nonthreatening therapeutic medium.

Art therapy is basically the use of art as a therapeutic means of expression. Some children and adults may express themselves better through art than through verbal or written means. It may involve viewing art and then exploring and sharing what it means to one's self. Or it may entail actually creating art at home or in session using media such as clay, paint, chalk, and the like (Barker, 2003). Creativity and freedom of expression may be fostered through providing a wide variety of art materials with which to work (Josephs, 2005). Artwork may be discussed within the context of therapeutic groups or with an individual's therapist. Also, the process of creating the art can be cathartic in and of itself. Encouraging the pursuit of creative activities such as painting and sculpting potentially relieves stress while simultaneously promoting positive self-care (Geldard, 2009). Some children will prefer to draw or paint their stories when utilizing storytelling techniques, enabling them to more comfortably express their emotions.

Control theory involves having the perception of control over one's environment and one's life (Glasser, 1984; Slivinske & Fitch, 1987). It has been renamed *choice theory* and supports the idea of being able to choose our behaviors (Glasser, 1998). Those who feel they have some sense of control over their lives, actions, and environments are more likely to feel hopeful and to have better problem-solving skills than those who feel they do not have control (Slattery, 2004).

As helping professionals are aware, children, especially those in the family or children's services settings, often have little control over what happens in their lives. They are brought to counseling because of divorce, abuse, parental addictions, and similar life situations. One of the benefits of this book is that therapeutic gains may occur simply by having the child complete or finish the ending to the story. In fact, more than one ending may be written, one opting for how the child believes the story will end, and alternatively, how the child believes the story should end in a perfect world. Many times, these endings will be vastly different, which may at times be representative of particular issues or conflicts in the child's life. By using this book, children may gain a sense of mastery over their environment by controlling how the story ends.

If preferred, the strengths perspective may be highlighted. This entails focusing not only on the challenges presented, but also the assets or strengths that a child brings to treatment (Barker, 2003; Saleebey, 2002). This could include anything positive within the child or in the child's environment. Possible internal strengths include intelligence, resilience, survivorship, athletic ability, sense of humor, and similar attributes. Possible external strengths include positive parental relationships, sibling relationships, teachers, friends, adequate housing, and other environmental resources. These strengths may be relied upon even in the most detrimental of situations.

Recognition of strengths by professionals contributes to feelings of empowerment. Ways to identify strengths include paraphrasing problem statements of clients and then asking how they are dealing with the problem. Therapists may also ask (or write, in the context of storytelling) how they have handled concerns in the past, and assist the clients in applying lessons learned, skills, and abilities to current life situations. This allows for a change of focus and shift in perspective toward positive abilities and coping (Slattery, 2004).

The activities in the book that address strengths and/or fun/happiness may be used with many children, who have various problems, to highlight what is positive in their lives. The strengths may serve as a starting point to build upon toward positive change. Long-term resilience may also be fostered. Additional suggestions for applying the strengths perspective toward therapeutic storytelling with children are provided in the next chapter.

In the university setting, educators using this book would have the opportunity to demonstrate the actual application of these theories in the classroom setting. Students could form groups and role-play using the different theories, therapies, and techniques mentioned above. Typical developmental issues of middle childhood as well as risks and resiliencies could be identified and discussed using this book.

CHAPTER 3

The Strengths Approach to Storytelling with Children

Working with children who have multiple problems can be a highly emotional experience, which at times may contribute to feeling discouraged and overwhelmed (Williams, 2009). Also, children may sometimes feel overwhelmed with life's adversities. If this happens, one option is to refocus and redirect the energy of both the practitioner and the child toward the positive—past, present, and future. Acknowledge and deal with the hurt in a child's life, but also think about and envision possibilities.

Many mental health workers have begun to shift toward concentrating on strengths of children and families instead of focusing on deficits or pathology. For some professionals, this alteration of their therapeutic practice may be a difficult process (Helton & Smith, 2004). Practitioners may need to change their own frames of mind or worldviews regarding their child clients. Professionals must allow themselves and their child clients to dream and imagine better times, and to reflect on when times were "good." Also, redirect the focus toward what is "good" today in the child's life and what may be "good" tomorrow.

Building on the positive aspects of a child's life can enhance the therapeutic relationship (Crenshaw, 2008) and prevent future difficulties in a child's life. It is important not to minimize a child's pain, however. Directing attention to the strengths in a child's life also will help him or her to deal with current life challenges. Praising assets of children such as bravery, honesty, and a positive attitude promotes resilience of children at risk. Fostering resilience in children by focusing on the positive qualities and assets in themselves, their families, their schools, and their communities contributes to prevention and amelioration of maladaptive behaviors (Terjesen, Jacofsky, Froh, & DiGiuseppe, 2004).

It is imperative, however, to avoid trivialization of children's emotional pain or trauma in this process of discovery. For instance, if children have been affected by traumatic events involving violence or abuse, it is recommended that practitioners respect their pain and let them retain their right to process their feelings in their own time. Do not rush too quickly into identifying strengths before clients are ready, as this may contribute to their feeling unheard, uncared for, or disrespected. Give proper and full attention to the situations, challenges, and presenting problems, as well as the emotions and thoughts surrounding these, as these initially bring clients to treatment. However, when practitioners feel clients are ready, coping or survival mechanisms may be identified or reframed as strengths (Miley, O'Melia, & DuBois, 2004).

When searching for strengths, be creative and cognizant that these are not always apparent. Look for strengths everywhere, realizing that these may be built upon to find solutions to problems. Identifying strengths can function as a positive intervention in itself. When recognition of strengths occurs, this may free clients to further examine and express their thoughts and emotions, especially about the positive aspects of themselves. This, in turn, opens a door for the formulation of a positive plan toward change (Miley et al., 2004).

For example, a child who is performing poorly academically may be very sociable and considered a "class clown," which may cause him or her to experience negative consequences in the school setting. At first glance, his or her excessive talking and joking are negative behaviors. However, they actually may be very adaptive and could serve a positive purpose later in life. If the practitioner identifies sociability and a positive sense of humor as strengths, these may then be approached in a different manner. Perhaps expression of these strengths could be rechanneled into more appropriate venues, such as performing a stand-up comedy act during the school's annual talent show or performing in a comedic play.

Also, practitioners and their respective organizations must alter their way of viewing clients. They must switch from a pathology-driven framework to a framework that views clients in a positive light, which emphasizes potential. This shift in perspective will assist clients in seeing themselves in a more positive manner (Hepworth, Rooney, Rooney, Strom-Gottfried, & Larsen, 2006). Possessing positive coping skills in times of adversity or oppression, or the willingness to learn such skills, could be considered strengths. Explore with children and families how they have overcome difficulties and what has worked for them or someone they know in the past when faced with difficult situations (Miley et al., 2004).

One benefit of using the storytelling activities included in this book is that the stories help to normalize challenging events of childhood, instead of focusing on child pathology. Using a positive psychology focus, the practitioner may choose to promote resilience and empowerment and look beyond survivorship, toward fully developing the potentially thriving child. Even when children have experienced several negative situational life events such as death, abuse, poverty, and illness, great potential still exists in those children's lives and futures.

When utilizing the activities in this book, therapists may incorporate their positive attitudes into storytelling by selecting the positive features about the major and minor characters in the stories. If positive features about the characters cannot be found, create them. Therapists also may envision how the characters can be further developed. Additionally, strengths questions are integrated into activities throughout the book. Strengths questions regarding strengths identification as well as questions about coping with, dealing with, and handling situations allow children to explore positive, functional outcomes or solutions to theoretical as well as real-life situations. Examples of questions included in the activities in this book are:

- ➤ What are some things that he or she is good at doing?
- ➤ What are some good things about his or her family?
- ➤ What are this child's strengths?
- ➤ What did this child do right to make the day fun?
- ➤ What would have helped him or her to behave better?
- ➤ How could he or she deal with this in a good way?
- ➤ How does this person handle keeping the secret?
- ➤ How do you cope with being teased or picked on?
- ➤ How do you cope with your loved one's cancer or serious disease?
- ➤ What could help you to complete homework assignments?
- ➤ What are some of your strengths that helped you to cope with this situation?
- ➤ What did you do right to make it a great day?

The following strengths-based questions of Miley and colleagues (2004) have been added to, modified, and adapted to fit strengths-oriented storytelling with children. These are additional questions for the practitioner to ask himself or herself, which may assist in strengths identification when working with children:

- ➤ How does this child interact with other children?
- ➤ How does this child interact with adults in his or her life?
- ➤ What is unique about this specific child?
- ➤ What does this child like to do?
- ➤ What are this child's interests?
- ➤ What are the extraordinary qualities of this child?
- ➤ How is this child different from other children?
- ➤ How is this child similar to other children?
- ➤ What are qualities of this child's physical appearance?

➤ Who is supportive or "there for" this child?

➤ Who is supportive or "there for" this child's family?

➤ How has this child and his or her family or friends coped with adversity?

➤ What is this child's story?

Another concept worthy of contemplation is that one person does make a difference in the life of a child, perhaps especially a child who is facing adversity. This one person can be anyone—a teacher, friend, neighbor, social worker, or minister, to name a few. Common threads that have been found in individuals promoting change and resilience in at-risk youth include very basic qualities such as actually caring for the child and providing love and support. Showing true concern and interest are important as well, as is having high expectations for at-risk children and youth. Never underestimate how even one interaction may impact the life of a child (Benard, 2002).

CHILD Mind-set Tool

The following CHILD mind-set tool may assist practitioners working with children. It is designed to enable the therapist and child client to envision a "mind-set" for thinking about what is happening that is positive in his or her life. The CHILD mind-set tool is easy to learn and to teach to children with whom practitioners are working. The CHILD mind-set tool delineates the following mechanisms, strengths, abilities, emotional states, and goals of a child:

Cope with what life throws you.

Hope for change and better things to come.

Identify inner strengths from inside you.

Love yourself, life, and others.

Define what you stand for and dream.

The CHILD mind-set tool enables practitioners to teach the child to "go for the good inside and out." To use the tool, first explain its purpose by elaborating on each of the core concepts in the CHILD mind-set tool. Chapter 15, "Fun, Happiness, and Strengths," contains specific activity sheets that may assist in this process.

Cope

Discuss this concept by explaining to the child that coping with life events and challenges in a positive way is in itself a strength or a "good thing." It may be necessary to explain on a rudimentary level that coping means "how someone deals with or handles problems." In the stories practitioners create and finish with children, include examples of how characters have coped well with challenging situations. Then this may be taken to the next conceptual level by exploring how the child handles challenges and praising the child for positive coping both in his or her stories and in real-life situations. Examples of coping well may be provided, such as sharing life events and emotions with trusted friends, exercising, reading, journaling, meditating, focusing on life goals, and so forth.

Hope

Elaborate on this idea by explaining that hope is something that sustains people in difficult situations. It involves believing that change can occur and having bright expectations for the future. Practitioners may talk about times when they were hopeful, when the story characters were hopeful, when family members or friends were hopeful, and when the child has been hopeful. Consider how these examples have helped or may help the child in the future. Also, investigate and elaborate on what the child hopes will happen to him or her in the future, and what the therapist hopes will happen for the child. The therapist's expression of concern and hope will help to strengthen the therapeutic alliance and relationship with the child. When feasible, assist the child in writing and implementing a plan for accomplishing what is hoped for.

Identify Inner Strengths

Elaborate on inner strengths with the child by first explaining what they are. Inner strengths can be just about anything good or positive about the child. Examples include having a good sense of humor, intelligence, perseverance, survivorship in the face of hardship, faith in one's self or one's God, likability, kindness, a strong mind or body, or athletic ability. Practitioners should allow themselves to be creative and identify as many other strengths as they can think of together with their child client. Many children will need assistance with identifying their own strengths, so simplification of language may be necessary when discussing strengths. Strengths may be reworded as "good things" about one's self. Vary the use of appropriate language, depending on the developmental level of the child.

Love

Explore with the child client that love involves caring for others emotionally and treating others with kindness and compassion. Elicit from the child who he or she believes characters in particular stories love. Also, discuss who they think loves the characters in the stories. When the child is more comfortable with disclosure about himself or herself, discussion may then transition to whom and what the child loves, and who loves the child. Positive examples of ways of expressing love can be given, such as by saying kind words, giving hugs, or performing kind deeds. For some children, an expression of love may be as simple as gently petting a cherished pet. Appropriate examples of giving and receiving love may be modeled. Examine with the child the differences between feeling love or concern for a person and treating a person lovingly. The importance of loving himself or herself through self-care also may be explored.

Define and Dream

Depending on the developmental level and individual needs of the child, either the term *define* or *dream* should be used. For older children, define and clarify what a story character stands for or represents. Working with symbols enables children to more readily identify objects or symbols that represent what they stand for in their own lives. This may contribute to increased self-expression regarding emotions and life events (Crenshaw, 2008). It also serves as an opportunity for positive character building. The following questions may be useful in this regard:

➤ What does the character in the story believe in?

➤ What does the character stand for?

➤ What is a symbol that would stand for the character?

➤ What do you believe in?

➤ What do you stand for?

➤ What is a symbol that you would pick to stand for you? (e.g., a smiley face, a peace sign, a tree, an animal, a car, or other symbol)

For younger children, explore what the story characters might dream of becoming when they grow up, or what they might desire to happen in any given story. Explain that when a person dreams, he or she envisions goals, desires, and wishes for the future. When ready, the focus may then shift more directly to the child client, by investigating what dreams he or she might have. Answers will vary accordingly, depending on the child's developmental level. Younger children may dream of having a new stuffed animal, while others may dream of having more time spent playing with their mother or father.

When using the CHILD mind-set tool, remember to attempt to make the experience enjoyable for the child and, most importantly, focus on the child's strengths and on what is "going right" in the child's life. Remember to concentrate on the child's potential and abilities. This will promote growth and the development of increased self-esteem in the child.

Use of affirming language when employing a strengths-based positive psychology storytelling method is imperative. Alter the word choice, depending on the developmental level and the particular needs of the child. Language may also require explanations or changes when working with children from different cultures or subcultures. When using strengths-based storytelling techniques the following terms and phrases which represent encouraging language may be used:

➤ Kind, nice, good, strong person, happy, overcome

➤ Great potential, good listener, friend, lovable, doing better

➤ Athletic, smart, a true individual, unique, talented, artistic

➤ Great writer, creative, brave, talkative, sociable

➤ Good storyteller, skillful, competent, nice, happy, smiley, fun

➤ Determined, resourceful, assertive, you rock, a great BFF (best friend forever)

➤ Flexible, bounce back, resilient, clever, honest, helper

➤ Friend of animals, friend of nature, good child, great kid, proud

➤ Texting expert, computer expert, excellent gamer, winner

➤ Good grade, a person who tries, a person who does not give up

➤ It is OK, good try, don't give up, a person who is a leader

One theory of intelligence that may be helpful to practitioners when identifying children's strengths is Howard Gardner's (1983) Theory of Multiple Intelligences. He has encouraged the application of his theory in school settings (H. Gardner, 2009). The theory also is particularly relevant to finding strengths in children. When identifying strengths in children, bear in mind that everyone has different abilities, assets, and talents that are present in diverse life domains. These strengths may be built upon to increase positive feelings of well-being within the child and to increase feelings of positive regard from adults and peers.

Howard Gardner's (1983, 1993, 2009) theory points to at least eight types of intelligences or "strengths" that individuals may possess and that contribute to our humanity. A simplified summary of this theory follows:

➤ *Linguistic intelligence*, which is possessing talent to use language (e.g., authors, orators)

➤ *Logical–mathematical intelligence*, which involves having strong skills in math, science, and logical reasoning (e.g., scientists, math teachers)

➤ *Spatial intelligence*, which entails having enhanced ability to maneuver in the physical world and strong spatial skills including using mental representations or models (e.g., architects, engineers, artists)

➤ *Musical intelligence*, in which individuals have genuine appreciation for and ability in music (e.g., singers, guitarists)

➤ *Bodily–kinesthetic intelligence*, which involves skills to use one's body in a positive way (e.g., basketball players, soccer players, pottery makers, weavers)

➤ *Interpersonal intelligence*, which involves having an understanding of others (e.g., psychologists, teachers, social workers)

➤ *Intrapersonal intelligence*, which involves knowing oneself (e.g., philosophers, writers)

➤ *Naturalist intelligence*, which involves a deep understanding of and appreciation for nature (e.g., gardeners, farmers)

Attempts should be made to understand the unique qualities and intelligences of each child. These specific types of multiple intelligences may assist practitioners in identifying abilities and strengths of the children they are counseling. These assets may then be integrated into the stories of characters as well as the children's own stories in therapy. Focusing on individuals' intelligences, strengths, assets, talents, gifts, and capabilities creates a shift from a deficit, pathology-oriented focus and redirects attention toward possibilities, potentiality, and growth in the current and future lives of children.

Attempts to foster resilience in children, families, and communities should be a crucial goal of those serving children. Resilience may be thought of as overcoming adversity and risk factors, and results from an interplay of risk and protective factors. Protective factors that may assist in resilience enhancement in middle childhood include having strong, supportive relationships with parents or guardians. When parents/guardians are involved in the life of the child, have basic rules for the child to follow, and encourage the child to achieve, this promotes healthy development. By assisting parents/guardians in building strong, positive relationships with children, practitioners are promoting the long-term health of the children with whom they work (Charlesworth, Wood, & Viggiani, 2008).

Professionals themselves may promote healthy development of children by encouraging children to become involved in positive group activities or interests such as participating in sports or joining clubs. These foster healthy peer interactions and in many instances facilitate prosocial behavior. Also, teaching effective ways of coping with life's difficulties can buffer children from the challenges with which they may be confronted. Connecting children with mentors or serving as a mentor to children also serves as a protective factor. Simply being a positive, caring role model in a child's life can have a tremendous impact on his or her healthy development (Charlesworth et al., 2008).

4

Developmental Issues of Children

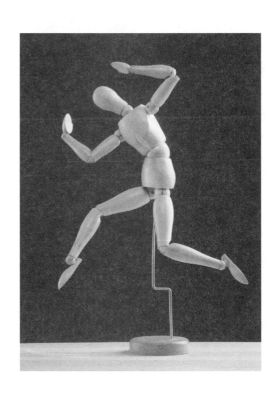

This book was written with the specific developmental needs of those approximately 6 to 12 years of age in mind. This being said, the important developmental needs and tasks of this particular age group are discussed below. It is imperative to remain cognizant of children's various levels of development as well as individualized variations in development when accessing the information throughout this book. Two well-known developmental theorists who have written extensively about this topic include Erik Erikson and Jean Piaget.

Erikson believed that human life involved the interplay among three very important systems—the biological, psychological, and societal (Newman & Newman, 2006). All three of these systems affect children's development during middle childhood. Children are changing more each year, as skills are refined and improved upon in the physical, mental, and social domains.

Biologically, children are physically growing, with many children approaching puberty near the end of this life stage. Body awareness increases, especially among girls. They may become self-conscious while experiencing these changes, and may benefit from education regarding hygiene and self-care. Psychologically, they are learning how to negotiate friendship and school demands. They also are increasingly gaining independence from parents and developing enhanced social skills and friendships while in the school environment. Children are now better able to articulate their own thoughts and emotions (Green & Palfrey, 2001).

Societally, they are exploring and testing ways in which they fit into the world and their social environment. They may face increases in peer pressure as well as academic challenges as assignments become more difficult in later middle childhood. Emotionally and socially, children are becoming somewhat more future oriented and are experiencing an increased sense of morality and empathy for others (Green & Palfrey, 2001).

Erikson, in his psychosocial theory, discusses the life stage of middle childhood, approximately ages 6 to 12, as a time when children face the normative developmental psychosocial crisis of industry versus inferiority (Barker, 1995; Newman & Newman, 2006). Industry involves the ability and desire to develop age-appropriate skills. Skills during this life stage often include abilities that are related to performing well in school and in various social interactions. If a child is successful at overcoming this developmental crisis, he or she will feel competent and capable. If the child does not overcome this crisis, he or she may feel inferior (Zastrow & Kirst-Ashman, 2010).

Feelings of inferiority may occur in instances involving child abuse, learning difficulties, divorce, and similar life events. Children with disabilities, both physical and mental, are particularly vulnerable. Feelings of helplessness may ensue when comparing abilities and skills to those of others in areas such as sports and reading. In general, those who feel very incompetent or inferior may become withdrawn from peers and family and may doubt that they have anything of value to contribute (Newman & Newman, 2006). This is why therapeutic intervention can be so important in these circumstances—to enable children to see themselves as industrious and capable instead of as inferior by building on their innate talents, gifts, skills, competencies, and abilities. Encouragement and support are essential components for the healthy development of children.

Jean Piaget also studied and observed children, including his own, who were influential in the formulation of his work. He was interested in the process of thinking in children, or cognition, and proposed a cognitive developmental model. His model spanned infancy through adulthood and elucidated progressive advances in alterations of cognitive processing. His four stages of development are: sensorimotor intelligence, from birth to around 18 months; preoperational thought, which begins when a child starts to develop language skills and ends at approximately age 5 or 6; concrete operational thought, approximately age 6 or 7 through age 11 or 12; and formal operational thought, from early adolescence into adulthood (Newman & Newman, 2006).

Most of the children using the activities in this book would fall into Piaget's category of concrete operations (approximately ages 6 to 12). During this stage, "the child can solve concrete problems through the application of logical problem solving strategies" (Woody, 2008, p. 112). The development of conservation also occurs. The child begins to think differently at this level. He or she is able to tell that an object can change in some manner, yet remain the same. For example, a child would be able to recognize that a ball of clay is still the same clay whether it is flattened like a pancake or is in the shape of a ball (Zastrow & Kirst-Ashman, 2010).

Children in the concrete operational stage often like to categorize items. One may notice that they enjoy collecting items such as baseball cards, rocks, balls, action figures, dolls, or stuffed animals. This is all a part of typical development. Classifying objects and cherishing collected items is common at this age, and children may find enjoyment and comfort in doing this. They are beginning to think logically (Zastrow & Kirst-Ashman, 2010).

Although still thinking at a concrete level, during this stage of development children often gain greater empathy for others and can understand another's perspective at a deeper level (Zastrow & Kirst-Ashman, 2010). Because they are understanding reality at a higher level, they also are able to better understand that negative events can happen to them and loved ones. Implications of this higher level of reality-oriented understanding are that fears of the unknown may arise. For example, they may be afraid that burglars will break into their homes and cause harm. Although great strides are made in development during middle childhood, most children will continue to think at a much more basic level than adolescents and adults.

However, be aware that child development occurs across a continuum, within a typical range of development. Thus, many children near the lower limits of middle childhood may still engage in fantasy play, and this may be expressed in their storytelling in therapy. Older creative children may do the same. Incorporate and encourage the further enhancement of this creativity when working with children who self-express in this manner.

During middle childhood, friendships become increasingly important, and many children will have best friends. Usually, friends will be of the same gender, serving an important purpose for promoting a positive self-concept as well as developing social skills for future relationships (Newman & Newman, 2006; Schmidt, 2001). They also feel a need to fit in with children their own age, and this appears to be happening at a younger age than in the past. Peer-group acceptance and adherence to norms of behavior become crucial (Charlesworth, Wood, & Viggiani, 2008). Friendship strengths and conflicts may be particularly salient during this time.

Fear of failure in school-related activities or sports also may impact children during this age. Pressure to succeed and drawing comparisons between their abilities and others may contribute to stress in children's lives. Adults in their roles as parents, teachers, coaches, youth group leaders, and counselors may promote healthy self-esteem by focusing on children's strengths and by helping to enhance their skills in areas that need improvement.

However, participation in team sports may be an important aspect of development for many children. Through organized sports such as soccer, softball, baseball, or football, children learn how to interact and work together in a positive way. They also learn how to follow complex rules and methods of interaction and interdependence. Through positive interactions in a team context, children may practice important communication skills that may be applicable to work and family experiences in their adult lives. Promotion of health and enjoyment of physical activity as an adult may be linked to playing sports as a child (Newman & Newman, 2006). In addition, positive activities in children's lives allows for less time for engagement in negative activities.

Social learning theory is also highly applicable to the developmental tasks of middle childhood. Social learning involves watching and imitating others' behavior, learning from this, and subsequently patterning one's own behavior after the actions of role models in one's life (Bandura & Walters, 1963). Thus, through their behavior, adults have the ability to influence the actions of children who are susceptible to influence during middle childhood. What adults do, both positive and negative, affects children's behavior. Children in middle childhood are likely to imitate the demeanor, mannerisms, verbalizations, and behavior of adults in their lives. Therefore, therapists, teachers, parents, and other important people in children's lives must be cognizant of their own behavior and their ability to influence children's lives (Newman & Newman, 2006).

Implications of social learning theory applicable to the real world include that children may imitate antisocial behaviors. What children observe in middle childhood greatly impacts their development in early and later adolescence. Thus, if children witness substance abuse in the family or neighborhood, one possibility for them is future imitation of substance abuse. This also applies to situations involving domestic and community violence. However, through the teaching of prosocial behavior and the modeling of positive, healthy interactions, children may learn and imitate healthier, positive modes of interaction instead of negative ones.

Lawrence Kohlberg (1969, 1976), another well-known theorist, focused on moral development. Many of the children using this book would fall into his levels 1 and 2 of moral judgment, the preconventional and conventional levels. Many younger children in middle childhood will be concerned with whether they will be punished or rewarded for particular actions, positive and negative, and would be categorized as being in the preconventional level of moral judgment. They may be concerned with negative consequences awaiting them for misdeeds, such as staying in for recess if homework is not completed. Other older children in middle childhood may be more concerned with gaining approval from authority figures. Thus, bear in mind that children in this age group are very much seeking acceptance of teachers, parents, and therapists, and are often eager in their attempts to please them. Furthermore, moral development occurs across a continuum, with some children achieving higher levels of moral reasoning earlier than others.

Robert Coles elaborates on moral development of children, noting the family as a major source of character development in children (Lageman, 1990). He writes that moral behavior is largely influenced by important behaviors of adults in the home and school environments, and that adults' behavior significantly impacts the behavior of children (Coles, 1987, 1997). This information reiterates the significance of promoting and developing positive role models in children's lives.

Also, child development is affected by cultural, religious, racial, gender, sexual orientation, disability, and ethnic differences. These are inextricably intertwined in the shaping and the essence of children's existence, including the time period of middle childhood. Practitioners must remain aware of each child's unique innate qualities, outward appearance, and situational circumstances, and respect the impact of these differences on development. Attempts to reflect on individual differences within one particular group must also be considered. Respect should be paid to diversity existing within the context of diversity.

Gibbs and Huang (2003) examine how child development is affected by ethnicity. Children's ethnicity influences their access to opportunities as well as expectations for behavior. It affects how developmental tasks of middle childhood are practiced and achieved. Interaction between those in the school and community environments with those of various ethnic backgrounds flavors how children concentrating on mastery of appropriate developmental tasks may be treated.

The context of ethnicity and other pertinent factors cannot be separated from the developmental process of middle childhood. Stigmatization by dominant groups based on race, socioeconomic status, gender, and ethnic backgrounds sometimes present additional challenges for children and their families to surmount in their developmental process of discovery and growth (Gibbs & Huang, 2003). Advocacy, in addition to traditional therapy, may be particularly relevant when working with those oppressed by a dominant group. However, professionals must remain vigilant in their attempt not to stereotype those from specific groups, and to look for apparent and obscured strengths within diverse children, families, and communities.

Many children in middle childhood will experience similar, characteristic developmental issues. These include the aforementioned normative school and friendship issues, general family concerns, and typical physical development. Other children who will benefit from the activities in this book will have many severe risk factors that have the potential to interfere with optimal development. These include domestic violence, child abuse and neglect, familial substance abuse, disability or death in the family, poverty, community violence, and others.

Hopefully, with help from caring professionals, at-risk children can be reached and redirected toward healthy development. The next sections in this book delineate key practice issues applicable to the lives of children. They also provide stories and activities relevant to overcoming challenging life situations, with coping and strengths-based activities integrated throughout the sections.

CHAPTER 5

Illness and Disability

Key Practice Issues and Story Selection

One of the challenges facing children today involves parental and family illness and disability. When illness or disability strikes one person in the family, the entire family system is affected. Unfortunately, illness or disability also strikes members of our youngest and most vulnerable population. Although children can be resilient and bounce back from illness and disability, it still can have a profound effect on their development. The fostering of resilience may be promoted by teaching healthy coping mechanisms as well as providing positive, caring adult role models in their lives.

In 1969, Elisabeth Kübler-Ross wrote *On Death and Dying*, describing the emotional and psychological experiences of people who are terminally ill. These emotional and psychological experiences can also be applied to other losses people experience throughout their lives (Kovacs, 2008). These stages are applicable to gradual losses suffered in various illnesses and disabilities.

The stages that Kübler-Ross has outlined are similar to the issues children may be facing when adjusting to their own illnesses or disabilities or those of family members. The stages of Kübler-Ross (1969) have been adapted to fit many of the emotions and behaviors children experience when coping with illnesses and disabilities in themselves and others. The following are the stages of death and dying adapted to apply to children coping with illness or disability in themselves or their families.

Stages of Childhood Adjustment to Illness and Disability

➤ *Denial*. The child denies that the illness is real: "I am not really sick." "Mom is not really sick."

➤ *Anger*. The child is angry that he/she or his/her family member is ill or disabled: He/she may act out angry feelings on family and friends. "I hate you!"

➤ *Bargaining*. The child may bargain with others or God in an attempt to change the illness or disability: "I will clean my room and act better if you make me better." "I won't talk back to Dad if you make Mom feel better."

➤ *Depression*. The child grieves for loss of health or ability of self or a loved one: "I feel sad."

➤ *Acceptance*. The child accepts his/her life as it is: "It is OK that I have cancer. My treatment will help me and I will feel better soon" or "I know my dad has a bad disease and can't play football anymore. Now instead he plays more video games with me."

The following stories deal with the issues of cancer in the family, cancer of a child, illness and disability of a family member, and the frightening experience of the arrival of an ambulance. Also, be mindful of the stages of childhood adjustment to illness and disability that the child may be experiencing. At times, the child may feel that the illness or disability is his or her fault, or express distress regarding disruption of typical family schedules due to medical treatments or doctor's appointments. Remember that the developmental level of the child will influence his or her reaction to illness or disability.

The story "My Mom" deals with the stress and anxiety that a child faces when experiencing the serious diagnosis of cancer of a close loved one. This story could be used with a child facing the serious illness of someone close to him or her. Coping strategies may then be explored with the child and his or her family.

"The Day the Ambulance Came" addresses the frightening situation of an ill loved one and the arrival of an ambulance. This could be used with children who have experienced sudden illness in the family such as heart attack or stroke. It also may provide an opening to discuss issues of fear regarding the arrival of ambulances, police cars, and fire trucks.

In "My Chemo," a child experiences feelings of illness and confusing emotions regarding her treatment for cancer. This could be used with a child who has cancer or another serious illness that involves prolonged treatments. The story allows for emotional release in the child and could be followed by teaching effective coping skills.

"My Dad's Disease" focuses on the complicated emotions involved when facing illness in the family. The child in this story misses the ways in which his parent previously interacted with him. He is adjusting to losses in functioning of his father, and with help from professionals may be able to find new fun and positive ways to play with his father.

My Mom

"Connor, Connor, would you please pay attention and answer my question," said Mrs. Robertson.

"Sorry Mrs. Robertson, I didn't hear you. What was the question?" sighed Connor.

"What is the capital of Ohio?" repeated Mrs. Robertson.

I know the answer, but I just can't think of it—too much on my mind, thought Connor. "I don't know," he answered.

"Columbus," said Mrs. Robertson in a perturbed voice with a frown on her face. "Please read your assignment tonight, Connor."

When I went to school today I knew what would be awaiting me when I returned home this afternoon on the bus. Today, my mom would find out if she had cancer. Well, I think I know the answer, Connor thought to himself as his Aunt Chelsea greeted him as he got off the school bus.

"How's Mom?" asked Connor to Chelsea.

"I don't know," said Chelsea. "We'll find out tonight when she gets home from the hospital."

Mom went today to get tests—MRIs, blood work, mammograms, and other stuff. "I hate tests at school," thought Connor. "I wonder if Mom hates her tests," he thought.

Mom and Dad got home that night around seven o'clock. Mom looked tired.

"Well, I don't want you to worry, Connor, but I have to talk to you. The doctors said I have breast cancer. I might need some surgery and some treatment to make me feel better, but I'm going to do my best to be OK."

Mom burst into tears. I just sat there and didn't say a word. I can't believe Mom has cancer. Suddenly I don't feel so well. My stomach hurts. "May I go to my room now?" was all I could say.

I just lay there and thought. "Cancer—that's not good. What if Mom dies? This really sucks."

Connor went to school the next day just like usual. Mom made his toast and got his cereal just like always. Somehow, though, Connor just felt different.

My Mom Activity Sheet: Level 1

Instructions: Write or draw the answers to the following questions.

1. Why is Connor having trouble concentrating in school?

2. How is Connor feeling and why?

3. What could Connor do to feel better about his situation?

4. How would you finish this story?

My Mom Activity Sheet: Level 2

Instructions: Write or draw the answers to the following questions.

1. Does anyone you know have cancer or a serious disease?

2. Can you tell me what it is like for him or her to have cancer or a serious disease?

3. How does this make him or her feel?

4. How does he or she cope with having cancer or a serious disease?

5. What is his or her story?

6. How would you change his or her story if you could?

My Mom Activity Sheet: Level 3

Instructions: Write or draw the answers to the following questions.

1. Does anyone close to you have cancer or a serious disease?

2. Can you tell me what it is like for him or her to have cancer or a serious disease?

3. How does this make you feel?

4. How do you cope with your loved one's cancer or serious disease?

5. What is your story?

6. How would you change your story if you could?

My Story: Level 4

Instructions: Write or draw your own story.

The Day the Ambulance Came

I remember the day that they came for my mom. I knew they would be coming, but I didn't know it would be that scary—all of the lights and sirens and stuff. I just sat in the living room and cuddled with my dog, Scruffy, while the paramedics carried her out on a stretcher. Mom was acting funny before they came. Her left arm and leg started to tingle and became numb. Then she started to cry. I didn't know what to do. I hope she is going to be OK.

The Day the Ambulance Came Activity Sheet: Level 1

Instructions: Write or draw the answers to the following questions.

1. What is wrong with this child's mom?

2. What might the child be worried about?

3. What was it like when the ambulance came?

4. How would you finish this story?

The Day the Ambulance Came Activity Sheet: Level 2

Instructions: Write or draw the answers to the following questions.

1. Has anyone you know ever been in an ambulance, police car, or fire truck?

2. Can you tell me what it was like for him or her when the ambulance, police car, or fire truck came?

3. How did this make him or her feel?

4. What is his or her story?

5. How would you change his or her story if you could?

The Day the Ambulance Came Activity Sheet: Level 3

Instructions: Write or draw the answers to the following questions.

1. Have you or someone you love ever been in an ambulance, police car, or fire truck?

2. Can you tell me what it was like when the ambulance, police car, or fire truck came?

3. How does this make you feel?

4. What is your story?

5. How would you change your story if you could?

My Story: Level 4

Instructions: Write or draw your own story.

Ambulance, Police Car, and Fire Truck Activities

Depending on the age of the child, the following activities may help the child release emotions about a potentially frightening event with an ambulance, police car, or fire truck.

1. What do ambulances, police cars, or fire trucks sound like? Act like you are an ambulance, police car, or fire truck.

2. Discuss the following: How did you feel when the emergency happened? Were you scared?

3. Imagine: If you were a policeman or policewoman, ambulance driver, or fireman or firewoman, how would you help people in an emergency?

4. Discuss the following: Name a variety of emergencies and discuss what an emergency is. Share examples of when and when not to call 911.

My Chemo

Hi, my name is Kaitlyn. I'm just like any other kid—well almost. I do have to go for chemo once a month. I suppose most other kids don't have to do that. Chemo is my medicine that is helping me to get better. It is kind of confusing, though, because after I take my medicine, I feel really sick and very tired. I can't wait until all of these treatments are over so I can start playing soccer again. I just want to be normal, and I really want my hair to grow back so Aiden will think I'm cute. My doctors say I only have two treatments left. I can't wait until they are over!

My Chemo Activity Sheet: Level 1

Instructions: Write or draw the answers to the following questions.

1. What is Kaitlyn worried about?

2. How does Kaitlyn feel?

3. How does Kaitlyn cope with getting chemo?

4. How would you finish this story?

My Chemo Activity Sheet: Level 2

Instructions: Write or draw the answers to the following questions.

1. Does anyone you know get chemotherapy or other types of medical treatments?

2. Can you tell me what it is like for him or her to get chemotherapy or other medical treatments?

3. How does this make him or her feel?

4. How does he or she cope with getting chemotherapy or other medical treatments?

5. What is his or her story?

6. How would you change his or her story if you could?

My Chemo Activity Sheet: Level 3

Instructions: Write or draw the answers to the following questions.

1. Have you ever had chemotherapy or other types of medical treatments?

2. Can you tell me what it is like to get chemotherapy or other medical treatments?

3. How does this make you feel?

4. How do you cope with getting chemotherapy or other medical treatments?

5. What is your story?

6. How would you change your story if you could?

My Story: Level 4

Instructions: Write or draw your own story.

What Does Cancer Mean to You?

Instructions: Write an acrostic poem using the first letter of each of the following words. Your poem should describe how you feel about chemo, cancer, and yourself or others.

C
H
E
M
O

C
A
N
C
E
R

What Does Cancer Mean to You?

Instructions: Write an acrostic poem using the first letter of each of the following words. Your poem should describe how you feel about chemo, cancer, and yourself or others.

Examples:

Crummy

Healthy—what I want

Energy—I have none

Miss my friends

Out of the hospital

Courageous

And I get to eat ice cream

Nice doctors

Can't stand it

End—can't wait until it is gone

Really sucks

My Dad's Disease

"I used to think my dad was a lot of fun," said Akim to his mother. "Now he is just boring. He doesn't play football with me anymore and he just always wants to sleep. He says that he's tired all of the time. He's just no fun anymore."

Akim just wanted his father to act the way he did before he got sick. He used to run and play, play football with him, and he even coached his soccer team. Now all of that was different.

His mom explained that it wasn't his dad's fault, but Akim didn't really care whose fault it was. He was mad and sad all at the same time.

He thought to himself, "Why can't I just have my old dad back? It's just not fair!"

My Dad's Disease Activity Sheet: Level 1

Instructions: Write or draw the answers to the following questions.

1. Why is Akim so upset?

2. How is Akim feeling? Why does he feel this way?

3. What could Akim do to feel better about his situation?

4. What are some activities or games that Akim and his dad can still do together?

5. How would you finish this story?

My Dad's Disease Activity Sheet: Level 2

Instructions: Write or draw the answers to the following questions.

1. Does anyone you know have a disease or disability?

2. Can you tell me what it is like for him or her to have a disease or disability?

3. How does this make him or her feel?

4. How does he or she cope with having a disease or disability?

5. What is his or her story?

6. How would you change his or her story if you could?

My Dad's Disease Activity Sheet: Level 3

Instructions: Write or draw the answers to the following questions.

1. Does anyone in your family have a disease or disability?

2. Can you tell me what it is like for your family member to have a disease or disability?

3. How does this make you feel?

4. How do you cope with your family member's disease or disability?

5. What is your story?

6. How would you change your story if you could?

My Story: Level 4

Instructions: Write or draw your own story.

My Dad's Disease Picture Activity Sheet

Instructions: In the space below, draw a picture of what you think Akim's father's disease looks like. Be as creative as you like.

My Dad's Disease Game Activity Sheet

Instructions: In the space provided or on your own, create a game that Akim and his dad can play together. Create game pieces to use with the game.

6
School Issues

Key Practice Issues and Story Selection

When working with children and families, it is common in practice to encounter problems or issues that children experience in school. These problems affect not only the child, but the entire family system. The issues focused on in the following stories include homework problems, possible learning disabilities or challenges, and bullying.

A variety of factors may explain why children are having difficulties completing homework. These include possible problems at home or school, including parental or teacher concerns. During assessment of the child, it is appropriate to attempt to find out what the contributing, underlying issues are and to attempt to ameliorate these during the treatment phase of counseling. Trauma and learning disabilities and challenges may also be factors for particular children struggling with homework. Yet, for others, the lure of playing video games, watching television, or texting friends competes with completion of homework assignments.

According to McDonald-Wikler, a learning disability can be defined as "a disorder in one or more of the basic psychological processes involved in understanding or using language . . . which may manifest itself in an imperfect ability to listen, think, speak, read, write, spell, or do mathematical calculations" (as cited in Zastrow & Kirst-Ashman, 2010, p. 142). Some possible effects of learning disabilities and challenges for children include "fear of failure, learned helplessness, and low self-esteem" (Zastrow & Kirst-Ashman, p. 144). The following story of Braden highlights these issues, and the activities address some ways to combat these negative feelings.

The story about Braden was chosen because it describes a child who desires to do well in school but who is having much difficulty completing his assignments. He also is receiving grades of D's and F's. His type of situation may occur in children who have learning disabilities or who have experienced a traumatic event resulting in impaired concentration. It also pertains to children who are experiencing basic homework difficulties unrelated to learning disabilities or trauma. This story may help to facilitate communication between the practitioner and the child.

Bullying is also a serious problem addressed in the stories "The Fight" and "Hanna's Dilemma." Various forms of bullying, traditional and nontraditional, currently influence children. According to Medline Plus (National Library of Medicine and the National Institutes of Health, 2009, p. 1), "bullying is when a person or group repeatedly tries to harm someone who is weaker. Sometimes it involves direct attacks such as hitting, name calling, teasing, or taunting. Sometimes it is indirect, such as spreading rumors or trying to make others reject someone."

In today's technology-oriented society, it may also entail the misuse of email, social networking sites, video sites, and texting. Children and adolescents may spread rumors or post unflattering pictures or videos about other children on the Internet. Technology-related bullying or "cyber-bullying" is just as serious as traditional forms of bullying. Children need to be educated about appropriate boundaries and etiquette regarding the prudent use of technology.

The story "The Fight" was chosen because it focuses on a direct form of bullying where Kiara is tormented in the school environment. It also addresses technology-related bullying. "Hanna's Dilemma" focuses more on an indirect form of bullying when she is not allowed to sit in her assigned bus seat. Both stories may be used in therapy to aid children who have been bullied to safely express their emotions. They also may be used therapeutically with children who bully to assist them in recognizing inappropriate behavior and in empathy development.

These and other forms of bullying affect children in various ways. It can contribute to:

➢ Anxiety

➢ Fear

➢ School avoidance

➢ Violence

➢ Suicide (National Library of Medicine and the National Institutes of Health, 2009).

Homework

"Braden, did you do your homework yet?" called Braden's mother at nine at night.

"Yes, Mom . . . I did it," yelled Braden from his room, even though he really had not done it—again. You see, Braden hated homework. It frustrated him. Most of the time he simply couldn't do it. It was hard—very hard—for Braden. He used to really try, but when he would turn in his assignments and just get D's and F's, he figured "why try?" So he just stopped trying. Now Braden constantly battles with his teachers and his mom. They just don't understand. He wants to do his homework, but he just cannot do it.

When he went to school the next day and he didn't have his homework, he knew what would happen. Mrs. Jones called his mother. He also knew what that meant—he would be on punishment for a week. No TV, no video games, no friends over—no fun whatsoever.

Braden knew what he would do. He said to himself in class, "I just won't go home tonight."

Homework Activity Sheet: Level 1

Instructions: Draw or write the answers to the following questions.

1. How does Braden feel?

2. Why can't Braden do his homework?

3. What would help Braden to do his homework?

4. Where is Braden going to go after school?

5. What might happen to him if he runs away? What could he do instead of running away?

6. How would you finish this story?

Homework Activity Sheet: Level 2

Instructions: Draw or write the answers to the following questions.

1. Does anyone you know ever have problems completing homework?

2. Can you tell me what it is like for him or her when it is hard to complete homework?

3. Why is it hard for this person to complete his or her homework?

4. How does this make him or her feel?

5. What could help him or her to complete homework assignments?

6. What is his or her story?

7. How would you change his or her story if you could?

Homework Activity Sheet: Level 3

Instructions: Draw or write the answers to the following questions.

1. Do you ever have problems completing homework?

2. Can you tell me what it is like for you when it is hard to complete homework?

3. Why is it hard for you to complete your homework?

4. How does this make you feel?

5. What could help you to complete homework assignments?

6. What is your story?

7. How would you change your story if you could?

My Story: Level 4

Instructions: Write or draw your own story.

Self-Esteem Booster

Instructions: Write or draw the answers to the following questions.

1. What am I good at doing?

2. What am I not good at doing?

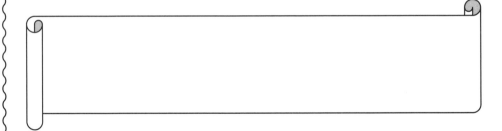

3. What do I want to improve?

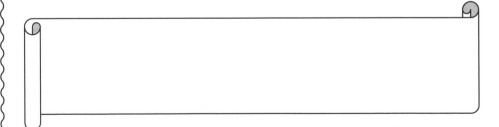

Homework Reward Chart

Instructions: Please place a sticker or a check mark in the box for each night homework or other behaviors are completed.

😊	Monday	Tuesday	Wednesday	Thursday	Friday	Saturday	Sunday
Homework							

The Fight

Kiara was tired of being picked on all the time at school. The kids picked on her for anything and everything she did. Yesterday, they called her a "nerd" because she didn't wear stylish clothes. The day before that, they said she was a "brainiac" because she got good grades. The day before that, a girl named Sierra dumped her chocolate milk onto her corn during lunch. The teacher even saw Sierra do it—but did nothing. That evening, Kiara saw horrible stories posted about her on the Internet.

Today, Kiara wasn't going to take it anymore. So when she got on the school bus and Sierra called her "fatty Kiara," she knew what she had to do. She grabbed Sierra by the shoulder and punched her hard in the face. Sierra was stunned. She fell to the ground and started to cry. "Now maybe they will leave me alone," thought Kiara.

The Fight Activity Sheet: Level 1

Instructions: Write or draw the answers to the following questions.

1. How was Kiara feeling about being teased?

2. Why did she hit Sierra?

3. How does Kiara feel about the stories that are posted about her on the Internet?

4. What else could she have done to handle the situation?

5. How would you finish this story?

The Fight Activity Sheet: Level 2

Instructions: Write or draw the answers to the following questions.

1. Has anyone you know ever been teased or picked on?

2. Can you tell me what it was like for him or her to be teased or picked on?

3. How does this make him or her feel?

4. How does he or she cope with being picked on?

5. What is his or her story?

6. How would you change his or her story?

The Fight Activity Sheet: Level 3

Instructions: Write or draw the answers to the following questions.

1. Have you ever been teased or picked on?

2. Can you tell me what it is like for you when you are teased or picked on?

3. How does this make you feel?

4. How do you cope with being teased or picked on?

5. What is your story?

6. How would you change your story if you could?

My Story: Level 4

Instructions: Write or draw your own story.

Bullying Quiz Activity Sheet

Instructions: Answer the following questions by circling T for True and F for False.

1. It is bullying if someone purposely trips you in front of a room full of people.

   T or F

2. It is bullying if someone accidentally trips you.

   T or F

3. It is bullying if someone sends mean and untrue text messages about you to other kids at school.

   T or F

4. It is bullying if someone talks to you directly about how you hurt his or her feelings.

   T or F

5. It is bullying if someone calls you a loser or idiot for no reason.

   T or F

6. It is bullying if someone posts embarrassing pictures of you on the Internet.

   T or F

7. It is bullying if someone asks you if he can post funny pictures of you on the Internet.

   T or F

8. It is bullying if someone teases you about wearing glasses.

   T or F

9. It is bullying if someone punches you or starts a fight with you.

   T or F

Answers: 1. T 2. F 3. T 4. F 5. T 6. T 7. F 8. T 9. T

Hanna's Dilemma

"I don't feel well. I have a stomachache," said Hanna to her mother. Hanna really did have a stomachache—from nerves.

"I don't want to ride the bus today. I know what will happen," she thought. "I'll get on the bus and Megan will be waiting for me."

Well, Hanna's mother checked her for a fever, but she didn't have one. Hanna persisted that her stomach really hurt, because it really did hurt because of Megan. Her mother finally let her stay home. Hanna was so relieved. She loved staying home with Mom and watching cartoons on a school day. Her mom always made her tea and toast to make her feel better.

Hanna and her mother did have a great day just relaxing at home. Her stomachache finally did go away—at least until the next morning, when Hanna thought about Megan teasing her on the bus again. This time, her mother made her go to school.

When Hanna got on the bus, it started all over again. Megan was sitting in Hanna's assigned seat and would not let Hanna sit down. Hanna asked Megan to "please let me sit down." Megan would not move. The bus driver yelled at Hanna to please sit down—so Hanna sat in another seat; then the driver yelled at Hanna for sitting in the wrong seat. Hanna felt like crying. Finally, Megan got up and let Hanna sit down in her seat.

"You big baby," said Megan with a snotty tone to Hanna.

Hanna sat there saying nothing. Her stomachache was back. "What a way to start the day," she thought.

Hanna's Dilemma Activity Sheet: Level 1

Instructions: Write or draw the answers to the following questions.

1. What problem is Hanna having?

2. How is Hanna feeling?

3. What should Hanna do?

4. Who could Hanna talk with about this problem?

5. How would you finish this story?

Hanna's Dilemma Activity Sheet: Level 2

Instructions: Write or draw the answers to the following questions.

1. Has anyone you know ever been bullied? Has anyone you know ever been a bully?

2. Can you tell me what it is like for him or her to be bullied? Can you tell me what it is like for him or her to be a bully?

3. How does this make him or her feel?

4. How does he or she cope with being bullied? What could he or she do instead of being a bully?

5. What is his or her story?

6. How would you change his or her story if you could?

Hanna's Dilemma Activity Sheet: Level 3

Instructions: Write or draw the answers to the following questions.

1. Have you ever been bullied? Have you ever been a bully?

2. Can you tell me what it is like for you to be bullied? Can you tell me what it is like for you to be a bully?

3. How does this make you feel?

4. How do you cope with being bullied? What could you do instead of being a bully?

5. What is your story?

6. How would you change your story if you could?

My Story: Level 4

Instructions: Write or draw your own story.

CHAPTER 7

Anger and Behavioral Issues

Key Practice Issues and Story Selection

Both anger and behavioral issues are common reasons for children to enter into a therapeutic relationship. A strong connection has been made between problems in the family and children's behavior (Hutchison, 2008). Unmanaged anger or behavioral issues may arise in a child for a variety of reasons. Existence of family problems in the home such as domestic violence or child abuse may contribute to acting-out behaviors. In these situations the child may be imitating aggressive or other negative behaviors.

Misbehavior also may occur if he or she has experienced a traumatic event. Children may be unable to directly communicate their emotions and may act out instead of expressing themselves verbally. Storytelling may aid them in articulating their feelings in an emotionally safe atmosphere. Through self-expression and the teaching of positive, healthy, nonviolent interactions, improvements in behavior may be seen.

Certain well-intentioned parenting modalities may inadvertently encourage acting-out behaviors. Children also may misbehave when they have overly permissive parents who allow them to do or have whatever they want whenever they want. These children may be crying out for age-appropriate limits. Working with their parents to improve their parenting style also will help the children. Information about the following parenting styles may be helpful when working with families who are having difficulty setting appropriate limits for their children:

> The Authoritarian Parenting Style is usually harsh and inflexible. It can feel cold and may involve hitting or spanking. Reasons for rules are not explained to the children.

> The Authoritative Parenting Style is usually more flexible, with less rigid rules. This style rewards good behavior and sets reasonable limits for the children. Reasons for the rules are explained to the children. This parenting style is believed to be the most positive and helps to manage behavior.

> The Permissive Parenting Style allows children to make too many of their own decisions without parental involvement. Clear rules or limits are not set, although the parents are caring toward their children (Baumrind, 1971).

In the therapeutic setting, it would be desirable to work toward the Authoritative Parenting Style with the family or guardians. This parenting style can help in managing behavior problems of the child through alterations in family interactions. This information may be shared with parents or parental figures in the child's life to facilitate change.

Sometimes it is unknown upon presentation what is occurring in the child's life to contribute to aggressive or uncontrolled behavior. However, practitioners do realize that destructive behaviors must be managed. Management of aggression is vital as a means of violence prevention. The following stories and activities serve as starting points to improve negative behaviors and anger issues. Practitioners may teach how inappropriate, aggressive actions may be replaced with appropriate, nonviolent conduct.

The story "The Angry Day" is about a child experiencing difficulty appropriately managing his anger. He is yelling, hitting the wall, and not obeying adults. This story would be helpful when working with children who are acting out in order to discover more positive ways of behaving. Interactive role-plays of positive social interactions could serve as models for the child to imitate.

"Bad Behavior" focuses on the problem of a child disobeying and not listening to the direct requests of adults. This story also can be useful with children who are acting out or who are used to having very permissive rules in the household. Again, positive ways of interacting would then need to be modeled and discussed with the child.

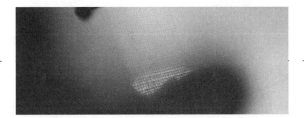

The Angry Day

"I feel so angry today. It's one of those days where everything just went wrong. I wish I could just punch something or somebody," thought Jordan.

He didn't really know exactly why he was angry—he just was. When he got home after school, he yelled at his little sister for getting in his way. She felt badly and started crying. His mother told him to go outside for a while, so he did. His neighbor Miguel came over to say hi. When Miguel said something he didn't like, Jordan knocked down his bike. When his mother called him in for dinner, he came only after she called him three times. When he found out what his family was having for dinner, he said, "I hate spaghetti."

He refused to eat his supper, so his mother sent him to his room. This just made Jordan even angrier, so he punched the wall.

The Angry Day Activity Sheet: Level 1

Instructions: Write or draw the answers to the following questions.

1. Why is Jordan so angry?

2. Is his behavior good?

3. How does his behavior make other people feel?

4. What could Jordan do to feel less angry and to behave better?

5. How would you finish this story?

The Angry Day Activity Sheet: Level 2

Instructions: Write or draw the answers to the following questions.

1. Has anyone you know ever been very angry?

2. Can you tell me what it is like for him or her to be so angry?

3. How does this make him or her feel?

4. What could he or she do to control his or her angry feelings?

5. What is his or her story?

6. How would you change his or her story if you could?

The Angry Day Activity Sheet: Level 3

Instructions: Write or draw the answers to the following questions.

1. Have you ever been very angry?

2. Can you tell me what it is like for you when you are angry?

3. How does this make you feel?

4. What could you do to control your angry feelings?

5. What is your story?

6. How would you change your story if you could?

My Story: Level 4

Instructions: Write or draw your own story.

Anger Activity Sheet: Hitting

Instructions: I am allowed to punch or hit at certain times. I am not allowed to punch or hit at certain times. Complete the following statements.

1. I can punch or hit when I:

2. I cannot punch or hit when:

3. There are consequences for punching or hitting. If I punch or hit, I will be in trouble with my:

   Who else could I hurt if I punch or hit?

4. Let's practice when it's OK to punch or hit!

Anger Activity Sheet: Hitting

Possible Answer Sheet

Instructions: I am allowed to punch or hit at certain times. I am not allowed to punch or hit at certain times.
   Possible Answers:

1. I can punch or hit when I: use a punching bag, am hitting a pillow to express my anger, am hitting a punch ball, am beating on the drums, am boxing, am defending myself

2. I cannot punch or hit when: I am mad at someone, I want to pick on someone, I want to feel better than others

3. There are consequences for punching or hitting. If I punch or hit, I will be in trouble with my: parents, teachers, principal, the police, and others

   Who else could I hurt if I hit or punch? The person I hit, myself, my family

4. Let's practice when it's OK to punch or hit!
   a. Practice safely hitting a pillow.
   b. Practice beating a drum to relax.
   c. Hit a punch ball to release your anger.
   d. Hit a whiffle ball with a plastic bat.

Bad Behavior

Trevor was tired, it was late, and he was playing outside at the neighbor's house. He liked playing there, but he did not like being told what to do. He enjoyed picking crabapples from his neighbor's tree and throwing them as hard as he could down the drive with Caleb, his neighbor. Sometimes he threw them into the road when no one was looking. He knew he wasn't supposed to, but he did not care. So, tonight, he threw them into the road anyway.

Mrs. Steel, Caleb's mother, had seen Trevor throw the crabapples as she watched from the window as the boys played. She came outside and asked Trevor to please stop throwing the crabapples.

"I don't have to listen to you," said Trevor, "you're not my mother."

"Then you'll have to go home, Trevor, and play at your own house," replied Mrs. Steel.

"I'm not leaving," said Trevor.

"Then I'll have to call your mother to take you home," said Mrs. Steel in a firm voice.

"I don't care if you call my mother. Go ahead," said Trevor.

So Mrs. Steel did call Trevor's mother, and she came and took him home.

Bad Behavior Activity Sheet: Level 1

Instructions: Write or draw the answers to the following questions.

1. Why was Trevor acting so poorly?

2. How did Trevor's behavior make Mrs. Steel feel?

3. Should Trevor's mother punish him? If so, how?

4. What could Trevor do to behave better?

5. How would you finish this story?

Bad Behavior Activity Sheet: Level 2

Instructions: Write or draw the answers to the following questions.

1. Has anyone you know ever had very bad behavior?

2. Can you tell me what happened when he or she had very bad behavior?

3. What did this person do? How did this make him or her feel?

4. What would have helped him or her to behave better?

5. What is his or her story?

6. How would you change his or her story if you could?

Bad Behavior Activity Sheet: Level 3

Instructions: Write or draw the answers to the following questions.

1. Have you ever had very bad behavior?

2. Can you tell me what happened when you had very bad behavior?

3. What did you do? How did this make you feel?

4. What would have helped you to behave better?

5. What is your story?

6. How would you change your story if you could?

My Story: Level 4

Instructions: Write or draw your own story.

Behavior Reward Chart

Instructions: Please place a sticker or a check mark in the box for each day of good behavior.

😊	Monday	Tuesday	Wednesday	Thursday	Friday	Saturday	Sunday
Good Behavior							

8

Social Adjustment and Shyness

Key Practice Issues and Story Selection

Many children will experience times in their young lives when they struggle with issues of social awkwardness, embarrassment over developing skill levels, and shyness. It is not uncommon for parents to be concerned about their children's shyness or lack of friends (Mize & Abell, 2009). Their concerns are not unwarranted. Children who are not accepted by peers may feel unhappy and alone. In addition, they may experience lowered self-esteem and depression (Asher & Williams, 1993). Conversely, possessing positive peer relationships may promote positive self-care and shield children from the effects of stressful life events (Geldard, 2009).

Practitioners can help to improve children's social skills in various ways. Suggestions for practitioners include the following:

➤ Social skills can be taught and modeled to enable children to be more confident in social settings. Role-plays may be helpful in this area.

➤ Assertiveness and boundary training may be practiced with the therapist (Geldard, 2009).

➤ Skills can be improved to build children's self-confidence, such as in sports.

➤ Coping skills can be developed to deal with disappointments and to promote resilience.

Additionally, social problem-solving skills may be taught and directed toward reality-based life situations. In conjunction with the practitioner, children may benefit from applying the following intervention techniques to their specific social adjustment challenges. This involves:

- Identifying the problem and its cause(s)
- Producing a list of numerous solutions to the problem
- Choosing an actual solution
- Attempting to implement the solution strategy
- Assessing the effectiveness of the implemented strategy in regard to functional outcomes (Harris, 2006)

The story "The Big Game" addresses the feelings of a child who is not performing well in sports and who is very shy and socially disconnected. This story would be well suited for the child who is not performing well in any area – sports, band, art, and so forth. It could be used in the practice setting as a turning point toward change. Application of the aforementioned social problem-solving skills technique is relevant to this story and many others.

"Mischa's Kitten" can be used therapeutically with children who are very shy. It touches on the idea that it is acceptable to be quiet and to accept yourself for who you are. It also serves as an opening for discussion about developing positive methods of interacting socially with others.

"Sometimes I Don't Know What to Say" attends to the topic of social awkwardness and timidity. This story could be paired with role-plays that model how to positively interact with others. Constructive social interactions could be practiced with a therapist.

The Big Game

It was Andrew's first year of playing baseball. He liked practicing with his mom and dad in the backyard. He could throw pretty well, but he wasn't so good at batting. So as the big game on Saturday approached, he really wasn't looking forward to it—especially since all of the other boys on the team knew each other very well. He just didn't seem to fit in. He was a quiet kid, and everyone else talked a lot.

On Saturday morning, he and his dad threw around some balls in the backyard to warm up before the game. He couldn't help but be nervous.

Andrew approached the plate three times that day, and he struck out three times. He could feel everyone's eyes on him as he walked off the field. As he sat on the bench, he heard his mom call out, "Good try, Andrew."

The Big Game Activity Sheet: Level 1

Instructions: Write or draw the answers to the following questions.

1. How is Andrew feeling?

2. Why is he feeling this way?

3. What could Andrew do to feel better?

4. What are some things that you think Andrew might be good at doing?

5. How would you finish this story?

The Big Game Activity Sheet: Level 2

Instructions: Write or draw the answers to the following questions.

1. Has anyone you know ever felt shy or embarrassed? Has anyone you know ever felt that he or she was not good at doing something?

2. Can you tell me what it was like for him or her to be shy, embarrassed, or not good at something?

3. How does this make him or her feel?

4. What are some things that he or she is good at doing?

5. What is his or her story?

6. How would you change his or her story if you could?

The Big Game Activity Sheet: Level 3

Instructions: Write or draw the answers to the following questions.

1. Have you ever felt shy or embarrassed? Have you ever felt that you were not good at doing something?

2. Can you tell me what it was like for you to be shy, embarrassed, or not good at something?

3. How does this make you feel?

4. What are some things that you are good at doing?

5. What is your story?

6. How would you change your story if you could?

My Story: Level 4

Instructions: Write or draw your own story.

Mischa's Kitten

Mischa walked next door with her brother Michael to the Mitchell's house. She had been waiting for this day for a long time. Tabby, the Mitchell's cat, had given birth to kittens, and now they were old enough to be given away.

Mischa had already played with the kittens several times, and she knew just the one she wanted. It was the quiet, timid, runt of the litter who always seemed to hide in the corner. It did not like noise or too much excitement. "It's kind of like me," thought Mischa.

Luckily, the kitten she wanted was available. She named her kitten Sweetie. At first when Sweetie was with Mischa in her new home, she would run and hide under her dresser. Mischa had to convince Sweetie to come out by talking to her very quietly and gently. Then she petted her ever so softly. Gradually, Sweetie would come out on her own. She started to like and to trust Mischa. Mischa always made sure Sweetie had plenty of food and water—and, most importantly, love. When Mischa went to school that fall, she made a special toy for Sweetie out of her old sock. She knew that Sweetie would miss her. Sweetie did miss Mischa, but she would carry her new toy in her mouth to make her feel better. When Mischa arrived home from school, she picked up Sweetie and cuddled her tightly. They both were very happy that Mischa was home.

Mischa's Kitten Activity Sheet: Level 1

Instructions: Write or draw the answers to the following questions.

1. How are Mischa and Sweetie alike?

2. How did Mischa help Sweetie to be less timid?

3. How would you help Mischa to be less shy?

4. How would you finish this story?

Mischa's Kitten Activity Sheet: Level 2

Instructions: Write or draw the answers to the following questions.

1. Is anyone you know ever shy or quiet?

2. What could he or she do to be less shy?

3. Has anyone you know ever gotten a new pet? What was that like?

4. What is his or her story?

5. How would you change his or her story if you wanted to?

Mischa's Kitten Activity Sheet: Level 3

Instructions: Write or draw the answers to the following questions.

1. Are you ever shy or quiet? What does that feel like?

2. What could you do to be less shy?

3. Have you ever wanted or gotten a new pet? If yes, what would it be like or what was it like to get a new pet?

4. What is your story?

5. How would you change your story if you wanted to?

My Story: Level 4

Instructions: Write or draw your own story.

Sometimes I Don't Know What to Say

"Sometimes I get so nervous," thought Mai. "I just don't know what to say around other people besides my family."

When Mai goes to school or to parties, she gets so anxious that she does not talk to anyone. She wants to make friends, but it is hard for her to even talk to anyone. She is a nice person, but she does not let anyone know who she really is. She really likes to read, play video games, and sing—but hardly anyone knows those things about her.

Mai thought to herself, "I wish I had a few close friends to talk to or to play video games with."

Sometimes I Don't Know What to Say
Activity Sheet: Level 1

Instructions: Write or draw the answers to the following questions.

1. Why is Mai so nervous and shy?

2. How does Mai feel about her situation?

3. How would you help Mai to be less shy and to make friends?

4. What are some good things about Mai?

5. How would you finish this story?

Sometimes I Don't Know What to Say
Activity Sheet: Level 2

Instructions: Write or draw the answers to the following questions.

1. Does anyone you know ever get very nervous about talking to people?

2. Can you tell me what it is like when he or she feels nervous or shy?

3. How would you help this person to be less shy and to make friends?

4. What are some good things about this person?

5. What is his or her story?

6. How would you change his or her story if you could?

Sometimes I Don't Know What to Say
Activity Sheet: Level 3

Instructions: Write or draw the answers to the following questions.

1. Do you ever get very nervous about talking to people?

2. Can you tell me what it is like when you feel nervous or shy?

3. What could you do to be less shy and to make friends?

4. What are some good things about you?

5. What is your story?

6. How would you change your story if you could?

My Story: Level 4

Instructions: Write or draw your own story.

Making Friends Activity Sheet

Instructions: Circle the following sentences that may help children to make friends.

Can I play with you?
What's your name?
What kind of things do you like to do?
I don't like you.
I don't like the shirt you are wearing today.
I like the shirt you are wearing today.
I like to go to movies, do you?
What kind of music do you like?
I think you are nice.
I think you smell bad.
Do you want to come over my house to play?
I will see you tonight at the soccer game.
Saying nothing.
Hiding in the corner to stay away from other kids.
You look nice today.
What kind of video games do you like?
Do you like to text?
What do you want to play?

Trust Activity Sheet

Instructions: Write or draw the answers to the following questions.

1. What does trust mean?

2. Who do I trust in my life?

3. Who can I tell secrets to in my life?

4. When are secrets good?

5. When are secrets bad?

9

Divorce and Parental Separation

Key Practice Issues and Story Selection

An issue frequently facing practitioners is that of divorce and separation. Parental discord, fighting, and eventual separation and divorce have profound effects on family functioning and on child development. In the United States, over 1 million children every year experience a divorce in their family (U.S. Census Bureau, 2006). As children of divorce become adults, past wounds may negatively influence their ability to form positive marital and family relationships (Crosson-Tower, 2009). With positive intervention, these wounds can be healed.

Children frequently encounter various feelings and behaviors during and after parental divorce or separation. These include:

➤ Feeling like they are to blame for the divorce

➤ Feeling torn between both parents

➤ Feeling angry

➤ Being in a bad mood

➤ Feeling responsible for getting the parents back together

➤ Displaying acting-out behavior

➤ Receiving poor grades in school (Cohen & Committee on Psychosocial Aspects of Child and Family Health, 2002)

It is important for children, parents, and therapists to work cooperatively toward helping the children in the family adjust in a healthy way to divorce. Wallerstein (1983) has outlined six tasks that children should strive toward accomplishing in order to positively adjust to their parents' divorce. These tasks are:

➤ Accepting the parents' divorce

➤ Letting go of the parents' problems and concentrating on their own issues such as school and friendships

➤ Learning to deal with losses such as relocating, less money, and less time with a parent

➤ Recognizing and dealing with anger toward self and parents

➤ Accepting the finality of the divorce

➤ Believing that he/she can have healthy relationships and a healthy marriage as an adult

These tasks may serve as goals in therapy. The therapist should stress that the divorce is not the child's fault and that both parents will continue to love the child. Even with supportive parents, the divorce likely will still be very difficult for the child to handle. Parents' resolving their disagreements in an amicable manner can decrease the stress level of the child.

The story entitled "Parents" describes the life of a child whose parents are fighting excessively and are threatening divorce. It describes some of the emotions and problems that a child may experience, such as conflicting loyalties to parents, loss of time and affection from parents, possible losses of friends because of relocation, and loss of home and neighborhood. This story can be used effectively with children who are about to experience a divorce or with those who have experienced a divorce in their family.

The story "The Fair" describes a wonderful day in which everyone in the family gets along and has great fun at the county fair. At the end of the story, it is revealed that the child's family is back together after a separation. This is a common fantasy of children who have experienced divorce and may be used with children who are experiencing repeated separations in their families or with children who are bearing the responsibility of trying to reunite their parents.

Parents

My name is Brandon, and my parents have been fighting a lot lately—way more than normal. At night I lay awake sometimes and hear them arguing. I wish they would just stop it. They tell me not to fight at school, but they sure fight at home.

The other day, after one of their big fights, my mom asked me who I would want to live with—my mom or my dad—if they got divorced. How does a kid answer that question? Do you think my parents will really get divorced? What will happen to me, I wonder? I love my mom, but I love my dad, too. Who would I live with? If I have to move, that would be horrible—all of my best friends live right in my neighborhood. No, I definitely do not want to move. I don't want my parents to get divorced, but I don't want them to fight all the time, either. What am I going to do?

Parents Activity Sheet: Level 1

Instructions: Write or draw the answers to the following questions.

1. How is Brandon feeling?

2. Do you think Brandon's parents will get divorced?

3. What will Brandon do if they do get divorced?

4. Why are Brandon's parents fighting so much?

5. How would you finish this story?

Parents Activity Sheet: Level 2

Instructions: Write or draw the answers to the following questions.

1. Does anyone you know have parents who are divorced?

2. Can you tell me what it is like for him or her to have parents who are divorced?

3. How does this make him or her feel?

4. What are some good things about his or her family?

5. What is his or her story?

6. How would you change his or her story if you could?

Parents Activity Sheet: Level 3

Instructions: Write or draw the answers to the following questions.

1. Are your parents divorced?

2. Can you tell me what it is like to have parents who are divorced?

3. How does this make you feel?

4. What are some good things about your family?

5. What is your family's story?

6. How would you change your family's story if you could?

My Story: Level 4

Instructions: Write or draw your own story.

The Fair

"I do love going to the fair," thought Ashley. She loved the rides, the music, the games, and, of course, the food. Who wouldn't love it?

"After Dad gets home from work, we are all going to the fair—Dad, me, and Mom. I can't wait."

Ashley's dad got home from work just in time. Ashley and her mother hurriedly put on their shoes and ran to the car.

The fair was as exciting and fun as Ashley had remembered. Ashley and her parents rode quite a few rides together, including the Ferris wheel. Then they saw the draft horses—Ashley especially liked seeing the tan one with its brand new foal. Someday, Ashley hoped she could work with animals, maybe as a veterinarian. The milking parlor was pretty interesting. Ashley even got to milk a Holstein.

Next, they all got to eat their favorite fair food. Ashley ordered fried cheese with sauce, Dad had a hamburger with fries, and Mom had a soft serve chocolate cone.

Before they left for home, Ashley played ring toss—which is next to impossible to win—and she ringered the bottle! She won a huge stuffed animal of her favorite cartoon character. It was so large that her dad had to help her carry it.

Ashley thought that this was one of the most perfect days in her life. The fair was great, but best of all, her mom and dad were back together. Everything would be OK now—they were a family again.

The Fair Activity Sheet: Level 1

Instructions: Write or draw the answers to the following questions.

1. What does Ashley like about this day?

2. How does Ashley feel?

3. What are some good things about Ashley's family?

4. What would your perfect day be like?

5. How would you finish this story?

The Fair Activity Sheet: Level 2

Instructions: Write or draw the answers to the following questions.

1. Do you know anyone whose parents are divorced or separated?

2. Can you tell me what it is like for him or her to have parents who are divorced or separated?

3. How does this make him or her feel?

4. How does he or she cope with the divorce or separation?

5. What is his or her story?

6. How would you change his or her story if you could?

The Fair Activity Sheet: Level 3

Instructions: Write or draw the answers to the following questions.

1. Are your parents divorced?

2. Can you tell me what it is like to have parents who are divorced?

3. How does this make you feel?

4. How do you cope with your parents' divorce?

5. What is your story about your parents' divorce?

6. How would you change your story if you could?

My Story: Level 4

Instructions: Write or draw your own story.

How Do You Have Fun with Family?

Instructions: Write or draw the answers to the following statements.
Fun with family:

1. When I am with my dad, we like to

2. When I am with my mom, we like to

3. When I am with my brothers or sisters, we like to

4. When I am with my stepdad or stepmom, we like to

5. When I am with my grandparents, we like to

6. When I am with my cousins, we like to

7. When I am with _____, we like to

Family Homes Activity Sheet

Instructions: Draw pictures of your two (or more) homes. List five things that you like and dislike about each home.

Lifemap

Instructions: Map the story of your life using the circles and arrows shown below. Use pictures and words to tell the story of your life from when you were born until now.

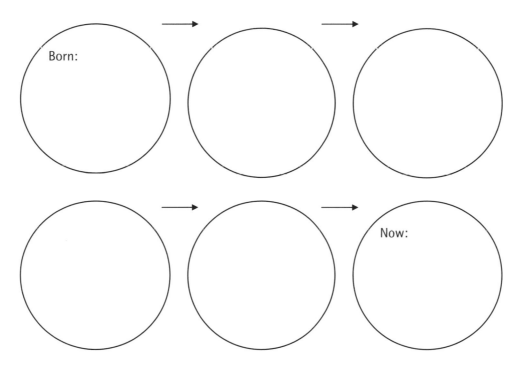

10

Domestic Violence

Key Practice Issues and Story Selection

Domestic violence is a serious problem that impacts not only adults, but also children. It is estimated that one in three children experiences direct observation of domestic violence between their parents at some time (Button & Payne, 2009). Children also may witness domestic violence in the home as a result of partner abuse in heterosexual or homosexual relationships, and from stepparents or mothers abusing fathers. Females abusing males does occur, but tends to be less common.

Domestic violence can have serious consequences for children's emotional and behavioral health. Some children may become fearful and overly passive, while others may model the behavior of the aggressor and become overly aggressive (Woody & Woody, 2008). They may also have difficulty with positive peer interactions. They may act out, and their self-esteem may be low (Button & Payne, 2009). As the child's therapist, it is vital to help the child who has witnessed domestic violence in the home to feel safe and to learn positive ways for men and women or partners in relationships to interact.

Emotionally, some children who have observed domestic violence may feel:

➤ Frightened

➤ Nervous

➢ Mad

➢ Sad (Button & Payne, 2009)

The story "Crying" was chosen for selection in this book because many children who have experienced domestic violence will relate to the feelings of anger that are expressed toward the perpetrator of violence in the home. However, a child may identify with the child in the story, the mother, or the batterer. Some children in domestic violence situations may not identify with the mother (victim), but may instead identify with the abuser (father). It is critical in both situations for the child to be taught that the violence is not the victim's fault and that the violence is not acceptable behavior.

The story "It's So Scary" addresses how a family copes with the stressful reality of violence in the home. Safety procedures such as hiding in a locked room and calling the police when necessary are examined through this scenario. Feelings of confusion and bewilderment are expressed, which many children may relate to.

In all situations, it is crucial for the therapist to stress that the battering occurring in the home is not the child's fault. This is especially important when working with younger children because they are more likely to feel they are the cause of or at fault for the battering, as young children are apt to be egocentric. With proper intervention, children can learn to develop appropriate, nonviolent social interactions.

Crying

When I got home from baseball practice I knew something was wrong. My mom was crying and her lip was bleeding. He did it again. I know he did. He hit her. You see, my mom's a really nice lady, and she doesn't deserve to be hit.

Sometimes I feel like I hate him. When I'm old enough, I'm going to really make him pay. Nobody—and I mean nobody—treats my mom like that and gets away with it—not even him.

Crying Activity Sheet: Level 1

Instructions: Write or draw the answers to the following questions.

1. Who could be hitting this child's mother?

2. How does this child feel?

3. What makes you feel angry?

4. How would you finish this story?

Crying Activity Sheet: Level 2

Instructions: Write or draw the answers to the following questions.

1. Does anyone you know have parents who fight a lot?

2. Can you tell me what it is like for him or her to have parents who fight so much?

3. How does this make him or her feel?

4. How does he or she cope with the fighting?

5. What is his or her story?

6. How would you change his or her story if you could?

Crying Activity Sheet: Level 3

Instructions: Write or draw the answers to the following questions.

1. Do your parents ever fight?

2. Can you tell me what it is like for you when your parents fight?

3. How does this make you feel?

4. How do you cope with the fighting?

5. What is your story?

6. How would you change your story if you could?

My Story: Level 4

Instructions: Write or draw your own story.

It's So Scary

Hi, I'm Keisha. I have a real problem and I don't know what to do. It's about my dad.

It's so scary when my dad does this. I just don't get it. He just goes wild and gets so angry. He gets mad about nothing sometimes. He starts pushing my mom, and sometimes he hits her. This makes me feel really upset.

When he does this, we all run upstairs and hide in the bedroom with the door locked. Then we hide inside the closet, too, in case he gets into the room.

Once, my mom called the police on him and he spent the night in jail. I felt badly for him, but I was glad he was gone.

I don't know what we are going to do!

It's So Scary Activity Sheet: Level 1

Instructions: Write or draw the answers to the following questions.

1. What is happening in Keisha's family?

2. How does Keisha feel?

3. What can Keisha and her family do to stay safe?

4. How would you finish this story?

It's So Scary Activity Sheet: Level 2

Instructions: Write or draw the answers to the following questions.

1. Has anyone you know ever had violence occur in his or her home?

2. Can you tell me what happened when the violence occurred in his or her home?

3. How does this make him or her feel?

4. How does he or she cope with the violence?

5. What is his or her story?

6. How would you change his or her story if you could?

It's So Scary Activity Sheet: Level 3

Instructions: Write or draw the answers to the following questions.

1. Have you ever had violence occur in your home?

2. Can you tell me what happened in your family?

3. How does this make you feel?

4. How did you cope with the violence?

5. What is your family's story?

6. How would you change your family's story if you could?

My Story: Level 4

Instructions: Write or draw your own story.

CHAPTER 11

Community Violence

Key Practice Issues and Story Selection

The community plays a large part in the healthy or unhealthy development of children. Nonaccidental violence occurs often in many inner-city areas where despair, poverty, corruption, drug dealing, and drug use are common. However, community violence can and does occur in nearly all types of communities, including suburban neighborhoods and rural communities. In 2004 alone, 2,825 children in the United States were killed by gunfire, which is higher than the number of United States military servicemen and servicewomen killed in Afghanistan and Iraq from 2003 to 2006 (Crosson-Tower, 2009).

Although individual experiences may vary, traumatic violence influences child development and may contribute to posttraumatic stress disorder, increased stress, and depression (Freeman, Mokros, & Pozanski, 1993). Hypervigilance, despair, anxiety, hopelessness, learned helplessness, and rage may also be present. The following suggestions may be beneficial when working with children exposed to violence:

➤ Children and families living in dangerous areas may need assistance coping with the trauma to which they are exposed, as well as help improving or altering their current environmental conditions.

➤ Children need realistic hope that their lives and those of their friends and family can improve.

➤ Children need their dreams returned to them so they can reclaim their rightful lives.

The story "He Shot My Brother" was selected because it deals with a child's feelings of anger, disbelief, grief, and despair surrounding the shooting of his brother in a drug-ridden, violent neighborhood. All of these emotions could be expressed in the therapy setting at the pace and intensity level suitable for each individual child. Hopefully, the practitioner would be able to work with the child and his or her family toward a positive, nonviolent outcome.

"The Shooting" was chosen for inclusion for similar reasons. It also concentrates on neighborhood violence and drug abuse, and the emotions surrounding these crucial concerns. Additionally, children growing up in a war zone may relate to the fear and stress experienced in this situation. Feelings of helplessness and confusion are exposed through the child in the story. Therapeutic intervention can help to facilitate self-expression of these feelings.

"The Shooter" was included because it confronts the terror and disbelief felt when violence erupts in what is often considered a safe haven—the school setting. These emotions can be released in a safe setting, and ensuing trauma can be addressed appropriately with the help of the practitioner. Supportive care may buffer children from tragedies while simultaneously teaching them healthy coping mechanisms in the face of tremendous adversity.

He Shot My Brother

Why did he have to shoot my brother? He was a good kid, and he was shot. He was just in the wrong place at the wrong time when the drive-by happened. It was probably done by the dealer down the street. If he can get shot, then anyone can.

What chance do I have in this neighborhood? There is always a lot of shooting and people using drugs. I am afraid to go outside.

I wish I could bring my brother back, and I wish I could leave this town—but I can't.

He Shot My Brother Activity Sheet: Level 1

Instructions: Write or draw the answers to the following questions.

1. What happened to this child's brother?

2. How does this child feel about what happened?

3. What is happening in this child's neighborhood?

4. What can this child do to try to stay safe?

5. What are this child's strengths?

6. How would you finish this story?

He Shot My Brother Activity Sheet: Level 2

Instructions: Write or draw the answers to the following questions.

1. Has anyone you know been affected by neighborhood violence such as shootings?

2. Can you tell me about what happened to him or her?

3. How does this make him or her feel?

4. How does he or she cope with the neighborhood violence?

5. What is his or her story?

6. How would you change his or her story if you could?

He Shot My Brother Activity Sheet: Level 3

Instructions: Write or draw the answers to the following questions.

1. Do you know anyone close to you who has been shot?

2. Can you tell me what happened when he or she was shot?

3. How does this make you feel?

4. What are your strengths that help you to cope with the shooting?

5. What is your story?

6. How would you change your story if you could?

My Story: Level 4

Instructions: Write or draw your own story.

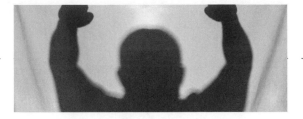

The Shooting

There's just so much shooting—I can't stand it. Sometimes we have to dive to the floor as the bullets go through the wall. Other times we have to find cover. I don't understand why this is happening to me and my family. We haven't done anything wrong. Why are they shooting at us? I wish the shooting and all of the noise would just stop.

Why doesn't somebody do something? Why can't anyone make it go away? I just want to leave this place and go somewhere that I can be safe.

I am just a kid—what am I supposed to do?

The Shooting Activity Sheet: Level 1

Instructions: Write or draw the answers to the following questions.

1. What happened to this child?

2. How does this child feel about what happened?

3. What is happening in this child's neighborhood?

4. What can this child do to try to stay safe?

5. What are some strengths of this child that help him or her to cope with the situation?

6. How would you finish this story?

The Shooting Activity Sheet: Level 2

Instructions: Write or draw the answers to the following questions.

1. Has a shooting ever happened to anyone you know?

2. Can you tell me what happened when someone shot at him or her?

3. How does this make him or her feel?

4. How does he or she cope with the shooting?

5. What is his or her story?

6. How would you change his or her story if you could?

The Shooting Activity Sheet: Level 3

Instructions: Write or draw the answers to the following questions.

1. Have you ever been shot at in your neighborhood or somewhere else?

2. Can you tell me what happened when someone shot at you?

3. How does this make you feel?

4. What are some of your strengths that helped you to cope with this situation?

5. What is your story?

6. How would you change your story if you could?

My Story: Level 4

Instructions: Write or draw your own story.

The Shooter

It was a normal school day just like any other. I said hi to my friends and was walking down the hall to go to my locker when it happened. I just couldn't believe it. At first I did not know what was happening. It all seemed so unreal. Everyone started to run and scatter in the hallway. A kid in school had a gun and was shooting. I was terrified. Everyone was running to hide under the cafeteria tables and desks. Some people tried to leave the building. I was able to run out of the front doors.

My friend Jake wasn't so lucky though. I saw him get shot right in the leg. It was horrible.

The Shooter Activity Sheet: Level 1

Instructions: Write or draw the answers to the following questions.

1. What happened to this child?

2. How does this child feel about what happened?

3. What is this child's school like?

4. What can this child do to try to stay safe?

5. How would you finish this story?

The Shooter Activity Sheet: Level 2

Instructions: Write or draw the answers to the following questions.

1. Do you know anyone who has ever experienced a school shooting?

2. Can you tell me what happened to him or her when the shooting occurred?

3. How does this make him or her feel?

4. What did he or she do to cope with the shooting?

5. What is his or her story?

6. How would you change his or her story if you could?

The Shooter Activity Sheet: Level 3

Instructions: Write or draw the answers to the following questions.

1. Have you ever experienced a school shooting?

2. Can you tell me what happened to you that day?

3. How do you feel about what happened?

4. How do you cope with what happened?

5. What is your story?

6. How would you change your story if you could?

My Story: Level 4

Instructions: Write or draw your own story.

Trauma and Child Abuse

Key Practice Issues and Story Selection

Child maltreatment is a problem for which many children and families receive treatment. In 2005, there were 3.3 million reported cases of child maltreatment. Of these reports, one half of the alleged maltreatments were substantiated (Medicinenet, 2009).

First and foremost, the therapist or counselor must ensure that, if a child is currently being abused, the abuse is reported to child protective services. Most individuals working in a professional capacity with children are mandated reporters of child abuse. There are various types of child abuse and maltreatment. Some of the common types of child maltreatment include physical abuse, sexual abuse, emotional abuse, and neglect (Child Welfare Information Gateway, 2008).

Various types of abuse can contribute to immediate and long-term effects, including but not limited to:

➤ Injuries

➤ Death

➤ Anxiousness

➤ Depressive thoughts and feelings

➤ Low self-concept

➤ Unusual sexuality

➤ Fearfulness

➤ Trust and relationship issues

➤ Aggressiveness

➤ Sleep problems

➤ Posttraumatic stress reactions (Woody & Woody, 2008)

Some points to consider when assessing whether a child has been physically abused include:

"Does this child get hurt too often for someone his or her age? Does the child have multiple injuries?" and "Are the injuries such that they don't seem possible for a child at that stage of development? Do the explanations given for the injuries make sense?" (Zastrow & Kirst-Ashman, 2010, p. 201).

When counseling or working with children who have been sexually abused or assaulted, keep in mind the following helpful recommendations:

➤ It is imperative that the child is believed.

➤ Listen actively and attentively to the victim.

➤ Do not blame the child.

➤ Discuss the abuse in a private location.

➤ Allow the child to express his or her feelings, including feelings of shame.

➤ Make it clear to the child that the abuse is the fault of the abuser, not the fault of the child in any way.

➤ When talking with the child, adapt your language to be age appropriate.

➤ Follow up on the issue with child protective services and appropriate intervention (Zastrow & Kirst-Ashman, 2010).

The stories and activities which were chosen may be applied to various abusive and traumatic situations in the lives of children. "Luka's Memory" was written to apply to both child abuse and other potentially traumatic events such as fires, tornadoes, hurricanes, car accidents, and shootings. It was purposely left vague so it could apply to numerous situations. This allows the child to vicariously address and express emotions about his or her own traumatic experiences.

"The Secret" can be used with children who are suspected of being victims of child sexual abuse or who are confirmed victims of child sexual abuse. Many times, victims will be lured into abusive situations by seemingly caring friends or relatives and are told to keep the abuse a secret. This story exemplifies this situation. However, the therapist should use his or her best professional judgment when interpreting discussions with the child, and use this story as one of many therapeutic aids. Also, remain aware that children who are not being abused may find having certain nonabusive secrets quite fun and positive. Thus, always rely on professional training when assessing for abuse in a child.

The story "My Family" addresses the feelings of ambivalence children who have been abused and neglected may experience. Although their biological family may have abused or neglected them, children still often care deeply for them. In this example, the child does not want to stay in foster care, but wishes to return to his or her biological family. This story provides an avenue for children to fulfill their wishes through storytelling, and enables them to express their emotions in a nonthreatening manner.

Luka's Memory

Luka remembered the night that it happened, but he wished he could forget. He thought about it every day and dreamed about it every night. Sometimes he would wake up at night sweating and could not go back to sleep. He remembered being so frightened that he wished he could just disappear or become so small that no one would see him.

"It was so scary that night. I just wish it had never happened. Then everything would be OK," thought Luka.

As Luka sat in school that day, he could not concentrate on his assignments. This was normal for him now, and his grades were slipping lower and lower. As he sat there, hearing but not really listening to his teacher, he faded into "Luka Land."

Luka's Memory Activity Sheet: Level 1

Instructions: Write or draw the answers to the following questions.

1. What could have happened to Luka to frighten him so badly?

2. What would you do to help Luka feel better?

3. What could Luka do to cope with what happened?

4. Has anything very scary ever happened to you?

5. How would you finish this story?

Luka's Memory Activity Sheet: Level 2

Instructions: Write or draw the answers to the following questions.

1. Has anyone you know ever been very frightened?

2. Can you tell me what happened to frighten him or her so badly?

3. How does this make him or her feel?

4. How is he or she coping with what happened?

5. What is his or her story?

6. How would you change his or her story if you could?

Luka's Memory Activity Sheet: Level 3

Instructions: Write or draw the answers to the following questions.

1. Have you ever been very frightened? Have you ever had trouble concentrating in school because of what happened?

2. Can you tell me what happened to frighten you so badly?

3. How does this make you feel?

4. What are some of your strengths that help you to cope with what happened?

5. What is your story?

6. How would you change your story if you could?

My Story: Level 4

Instructions: Write or draw your own story.

The Secret

Shayla knew that she wasn't supposed to keep secrets from her mom—at least that's what Mom said. "I promised Uncle Ron I wouldn't tell anyone," she thought to herself. She didn't want to break her promise. That was just wrong. And sometimes secrets are kind of fun and special. That's what Uncle Ron said.

Uncle Ron was really nice to her. Sometimes he took her places, like to the movies or the park. The other day Uncle Ron told Shayla that he was going to buy her something really special. Shayla knew she had to keep the secret now. She didn't want to let Uncle Ron down by breaking her promise.

The Secret Activity Sheet: Level 1

Instructions: Write or draw the answers to the following questions.

1. What do you think Shayla's secret is?

2. Should Shayla break her promise to Uncle Ron?

3. When is it right to have a secret? When is it not right to have a secret?

4. Is it ever OK to break a promise?

5. How would you finish this story?

The Secret Activity Sheet: Level 2

Instructions: Write or draw the answers to the following questions.

1. Does anyone you know have a secret? Should the person share the secret with someone?

2. Can you tell me what it is like for this person to keep the secret?

3. How does this make him or her feel?

4. How does this person handle keeping the secret?

5. What is his or her story?

6. How would you change his or her story if you could?

The Secret Activity Sheet: Level 3

Instructions: Write or draw the answers to the following questions.

1. Do you have a secret? Should you share the secret with someone?

2. Can you tell me what it is like for you to keep the secret?

3. How does this make you feel?

4. How do you handle keeping the secret?

5. What is your story?

6. How would you change your story if you could?

My Story: Level 4

Instructions: Write or draw your own story.

Trust Activity Sheet

Instructions: Write or draw the answers to the following questions.

1. What does trust mean?

2. Who do I trust in my life?

3. Who can I tell secrets to in my life?

4. When are secrets good?

5. When are secrets bad?

My Family

My family may not be perfect, but I do love them—and I miss them. You see, right now I'm living with my foster family until my mom can get it together. You know, she has some problems—but who doesn't? My foster family is all right, but they just are not my real family.

I miss my mom and my little brother, too—he's staying with another foster family right now. I know he misses me. I wish we could just be together. On weekends I get to see them with our social worker.

Before we were all separated, things really weren't so bad. At least I didn't think so. I just want us all to be together again.

My Family Activity Sheet: Level 1

Instructions: Write or draw the answers to the following questions.

1. What is happening in this child's life?

2. How is this child feeling?

3. How would you help this child?

4. How would you finish this story?

My Family Activity Sheet: Level 2

Instructions: Write or draw the answers to the following questions.

1. Do you know anyone who is in foster care or separated from his or her family?

2. Do you know why he or she is in foster care or separated from his or her family?

3. What is it like for this person to be away from his or her family?

4. How does this make him or her feel?

5. How does this person cope with being away from his or her family?

6. What is his or her story?

7. How would you change his or her story if you could?

My Family Activity Sheet: Level 3

Instructions: Write or draw the answers to the following questions.

1. Are you or have you ever been in foster care or separated from your family?

2. Do you know why you are or were in foster care or separated from your family?

3. What is it like for you to be away from your family?

4. How does this make you feel?

5. How do you cope with being away from your family?

6. What is your story?

7. How would you change your story if you could?

My Story: Level 4

Instructions: Write or draw your own story.

Family Homes Activity Sheet

Instructions: Draw pictures of your two (or more) homes. List five things that you like and dislike about each home.

Lifemap

Instructions: Map the story of your life using the circles and arrows shown below. Use pictures and words to tell the story of your life from when you were born until now.

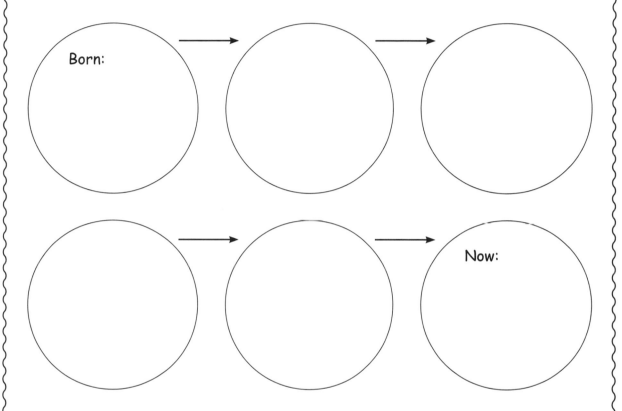

13

Substance Abuse

Key Practice Issues and Story Selection

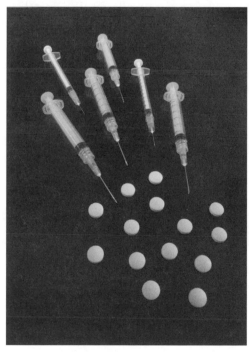

Chemical dependency and use is a serious and common problem in households in the United States. In the United State alone, it is estimated that up to 35 million children have a parent who is an alcoholic (Arman & McNair, 2000). It affects everyone in the household, including the children. We often hear of alcohol and drug use and abuse by parents and its effect on children in the home. In addition, when older siblings or other family members are abusing substances, this can have a detrimental impact on the child's development. Children raised in families with addiction may experience low self-esteem and have an increased risk of alcoholism and addiction themselves. Also, they may experience anxiety, depression, and acting-out behaviors at home or in school (Lambie & Sias, 2005).

Chemical dependency is a family problem. Various roles often develop in the dysfunctional family system, including the following:

➤ *Enabler*. This is the person who hides the substance abuser's use of alcohol or drugs. This is usually the spouse of the chemically dependent person.

➤ *Hero*. This person makes the family proud by doing well in school or other activities.

➤ *Scapegoat*. This child may act out for attention and use drugs and alcohol at a young age.

➤ *Lost child*. This child may be quiet and not demand much attention.

➤ *Mascot*. This child is often funny and relieves stress in the family with humor (Wegscheider, 1981).

The child may also display components of all of these various roles at different times in his or her development. He or she may be uncomfortable discussing issues surrounding substance abuse in the family. This may be indicative of feelings of shame and also fear regarding sharing the family secret with an outsider. Development of trust between the child and therapist is essential to the therapeutic bond.

The story "The Sleepover" was chosen because it highlights the stress that children experience when substance abuse occurs in the home. The child in this family is embarrassed, ashamed, and nervous regarding the substance abuse and violence occurring in her family. These themes could be used to allow members of families to open up about the dysfunction in their own families.

"My Mom's Problem" addresses parental alcoholism and its effect on children in the family. The child in the family loves his or her parent but is confused and worried about her drinking. He or she is also forced to prematurely act like an adult by assuming adult-like responsibilities, such as making his or her own dinner. This story would assist the child and family in expressing emotions surrounding familial substance abuse.

Therapists also may wish to review the following important ideas with children from families where chemical dependency is present in order to facilitate the development of positive coping skills:

➤ Chemical dependency is a disease that can be hurtful to everyone in the family, especially the children.

➤ Children can learn to cope with chemical dependency in the family.

➤ Many children grow up in families with chemical dependency.

➤ It is OK for children to receive assistance from helping professionals.

➤ Children are not to blame for the chemical dependency, nor can they stop it from occurring.

➤ Children growing up in families with chemical dependency are at risk for developing substance abuse problems. With help, though, this can be prevented.

➤ It is healthy for children to practice self-care and to develop positive feelings about themselves (Robinson & Rhoden, 1998).

Also, it is essential to support the child by stressing what is positive and good about him or her. Just having one supportive, caring adult who is genuinely interested in the life of a child can make a difference in that child's life and contribute to fostering inner resilience. Building on internal and external familial and community strengths may contribute to facilitation of positive change.

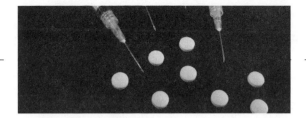

The Sleepover

It was late at night and the girls really had a great day. Joon really liked it when her friends spent the night. Shelby and Leesa were staying tonight, and she was very excited. They lay happily on her bedroom floor telling stories about the boys in their class. They all liked one cute boy named DeShawn. They chased him during recess and enjoyed playing with him. As they talked and joked happily in their sleeping bags, Joon heard her older brother Dakota come home.

"Oh, no," Joon thought. "I wish he had not come home. There will be trouble."

You see, Joon's brother is 16 and constantly in trouble. This meant a lot of fighting occurred between her brother and everyone else in the family. Joon did not say a word to her friends. She hoped they wouldn't hear what was about to happen. Joon knew what was about to come. She was embarrassed before it even happened.

"Where have you been," said Joon's father in a stern, angry, loud voice.

"At Devon's house," said Dakota in a slurred voice.

"What is wrong with you, Dakota?" screamed Joon's father. "You are high again, aren't you?"

The screaming continued for about 20 minutes. Joon's father angrily grabbed Dakota by the shirt. Finally, Dakota ran into his room and slammed the door, and the fighting stopped.

Joon just pretended it wasn't happening, and so did Shelby and Leesa. The girls talked a little bit longer about school, but said nothing about the screaming. Then they fell asleep.

The Sleepover Activity Sheet: Level 1

Instructions: Write or draw the answers to the following questions.

1. What is happening in Joon's family?

2. How does she feel about her family situation when around her friends?

3. How does Joon cope with her family situation?

4. How would you finish this story?

The Sleepover Activity Sheet: Level 2

Instructions: Write or draw the answers to the following questions.

1. Is anyone you know embarrassed or nervous about problems in his or her family?

2. Can you tell me what is happening in his or her family?

3. How does this make him or her feel?

4. How does this person cope with what is happening in his or her family?

5. What is his or her story?

6. How would you change his or her story if you could?

The Sleepover Activity Sheet: Level 3

Instructions: Write or draw the answers to the following questions.

1. Are you ever embarrassed or nervous about problems in your own family?

2. Can you tell me what is happening in your family?

3. How does this make you feel?

4. How do you cope with what is happening in your family?

5. What is your story?

6. How would you change your story if you could?

My Story: Level 4

Instructions: Write or draw your own story.

My Family Member: Letter, Text, or Email

Instructions: Write a letter, a text, or an email to a member of your family. You do not need to send it.

Dear _____:

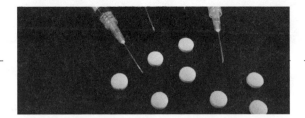

My Mom's Problem

I think something's wrong with my mom. I think she has a problem, but I can't tell her that. Sometimes when I come home from school, she smells like she's been drinking, and she's really moody. She'll be happy one minute and then screaming at me the next minute—when I haven't even done anything wrong.

When she's not drinking, she is pretty nice most of the time. We play video games together and she takes me to my soccer games. When she drinks too much, though, she changes.

I hate it when she drinks. Sometimes she falls asleep on the couch and I have to make my own dinner. I usually just make a peanut butter and jelly sandwich. It's pretty good, actually.

My Mom's Problem Activity Sheet: Level 1

Instructions: Write or draw the answers to the following questions.

1. What is happening in this child's family?

2. How does he or she feel about his or her family situation?

3. How does he or she cope with his or her family situation?

4. How would you finish this story?

My Mom's Problem Story Activity Sheet: Level 2

Instructions: Write or draw the answers to the following questions

1. Does anyone you know have a problem with alcohol or drugs?

2. Can you tell me what this is like for this person and his or her family?

3. How does this make them feel?

4. How does this person and his or her family cope with the situation?

5. What is his or her story?

6. How would you change his or her story if you could?

My Mom's Problem Story Activity Sheet: Level 3

Instructions: Write or draw the answers to the following questions.

1. Does anyone in your family have a problem that is very hard to handle?

2. Can you tell me what it is like for you and your family?

3. How does this make you feel?

4. What are some of your strengths that help you to cope with your family problems?

5. What is your story?

6. How would you change your story if you could?

My Story: Level 4

Instructions: Write or draw your own story.

14
Cultural and Religious Issues

Key Practice Issues and Story Selection

In middle childhood, children are usually trying to fit in and belong. This can be especially challenging for children and youth who hold different cultural or religious beliefs than the majority of the children in their school or neighborhood. Children also may be discriminated against in their own neighborhoods and schools, and as their ability to reason increases with age, they are more likely to understand that this is happening (Charlesworth, Wood, & Viggiani, 2008).

In the United States, children with different cultural traditions than the mainstream dominant Eurocentric, Christian culture may face prejudice and discrimination. Also, even if they are accepted by peers and teachers, they may feel isolated or unusual because of their ethnic, cultural, or religious heritage and traditions. These differences at times are highlighted in the school setting when class parties are held to celebrate dominant, traditional holidays in the United States such as Halloween and Christmas. Sometimes children who hold varying cultural or religious beliefs are unable to participate in these parties, automatically setting them apart from the other students.

In the story "The Holiday," a child is unable to celebrate a traditional holiday of the dominant culture in the United States because of differing cultural or religious beliefs. This story may be useful in practice with children who are experiencing a feeling of differentness or isolation due to cultural or religious reasons. The mental health professional may help the child by using activity sheets that highlight the positive aspects of one's culture or religion. At times, it may also be necessary to assist in educating classmates and educators regarding varying cultural or religious beliefs.

"They Make Fun of Me Because I'm Different" explores relevant emotions of a child who is humiliated and teased because of differences. The types of differences are purposely not stated, as children from various ethnic, cultural, and religious groups are often victims of prejudice and discrimination. Children also may relate to this particular story if they are different in any way. Other types of pertinent differences include being overweight or underweight, a child or child's parents having a different sexual orientation, being gifted, or having a physical or mental disability.

The Holiday

Sam waited outside of his classroom anxiously. He knew he could not celebrate the holiday today in the same way the other kids in his class were. It was his parent's wishes. So Sam obeyed his parents and did what they said.

His religion would not allow him to celebrate in the same way as other kids. So he went to another classroom with Mrs. Murray and colored with crayons while the other kids had their special celebration. He felt kind of funny about not celebrating with his class, though, like he was different from the other kids.

He did know that soon his family would celebrate their holiday together in a very special way. This made Sam very happy.

The Holiday Activity Sheet: Level 1

Instructions: Write or draw the answers to the following questions.

1. How does Sam feel?

2. Why can't he celebrate with his class?

3. Why does Sam feel different?

4. What are some good things about Sam and his family?

5. How would you finish this story?

The Holiday Activity Sheet: Level 2

Instructions: Write or draw the answers to the following questions.

1. Has anyone you know ever felt left out or different?

2. Can you tell me about what happened when he or she felt different or left out?

3. How does this make him or her feel?

4. What are some good things about this person and his or her family?

5. What is his or her story?

6. How would you change his or her story if you could?

The Holiday Activity Sheet: Level 3

Instructions: Write or draw the answers to the following questions.

1. Have you ever felt left out or different?

2. Can you tell me about what happened when you felt left out or different?

3. How does this make you feel?

4. What are some good things about you and your family?

5. What is your story?

6. How would you change your story if you could?

My Story: Level 4

Instructions: Write or draw your own story.

They Make Fun of Me Because I'm Different

I hate it here. Some of the kids treat me differently and make fun of me because I'm different. They call me names that I am too embarrassed to repeat. It makes me feel horrible. I can't help it that I'm different and that I am not like them.

I'm still a person, just like they are. Why don't they treat me better? I wish they would just leave me alone. It really makes me feel badly.

They Make Fun of Me Because I'm Different
Activity Sheet: Level 1

Instructions: Write or draw the answers to the following questions.

1. How does this child feel?

2. Why does he or she feel different?

3. Why are they calling him or her bad names?

4. How could he or she deal with this in a good way?

5. How would you finish this story?

They Make Fun of Me Because I'm Different
Activity Sheet: Level 2

Instructions: Write or draw the answers to the following questions.

1. Has anyone you know ever felt different or been called bad names?

2. Can you tell me about what happened when he or she felt different or was called bad names?

3. How does this make him or her feel?

4. How could he or she deal with this in a good way?

5. What is his or her story?

6. How would you change his or her story if you could?

They Make Fun of Me Because I'm Different
Activity Sheet: Level 3

Instructions: Write or draw the answers to the following questions.

1. Have you ever felt different or been called bad names?

2. Can you tell me about what happened when you felt different or were called bad names?

3. How does this make you feel?

4. What did you do or what can you do to deal with this in a good way?

5. What is your story?

6. How would you change your story if you could?

My Story: Level 4

Instructions: Write or draw your own story.

My Culture/Religion Activity Sheet

1. Draw or write five things you like about your culture or religion.

2. Draw or write five ways we can help other people to understand more about your culture or religion.

15
Fun, Happiness, and Strengths

Key Practice Issues and Story Selection

It is important in practice with children to focus not only on what is going wrong in a child's life, but also on what is going right. One theoretical framework that applies to this idea is the strengths perspective. This entails focusing not only on the challenges presented, but also on the assets or strengths that a child brings to treatment (Barker, 2003; Saleebey, 2002). This could include anything positive within or outside of the child.

Even in the worst of times in a child's life, there is usually something good that he or she will identify with or like in his or her life. These "good things" can be built upon as strengths. These "good things" can be anything. They can be a friend who sticks by the child, an aunt that he or she likes to call or text, a favorite stuffed animal who is always there for the child, or a loving pet.

Even in dysfunctional family settings, most people in the family will have strengths or "good things" about them. For instance, an alcoholic father may have a wonderful sense of humor and may take the children fishing. A mother who has mental illness and depression may bake the best birthday cakes ever when she is feeling well. We can never deny or minimize the "bad things" happening in a child's life, but identifying and discussing the "good things" allows professionals to promote resilience in children and families. It offers practitioners and the family something positive to build upon.

The story "By the Lake" was chosen because it highlights a relaxing and fun day that a child has with his or her family. They go to the lake and then stop for ice cream. The whole family is functioning well on this particular day, which is what practitioners want families to strive for. This story could be used with almost any child to help to identify positive interests and strengths of his or her family.

The story "The Great Day" was included because it portrays a child having a very positive experience in school with his or her peers. It draws on personal strengths, such as taking pride in one's personal appearance and academic skills. It also may be utilized with a variety of children to assist in identifying personal strengths and peer or school-related supports.

The story "My Friends" demonstrates positive friendships and peer interactions. These constructive interactions can buffer a child from negative life events and promote helpful, caring, positive interactions as children, adolescents, and adults. The story can be used in a fun manner to elicit strengths regarding friendships from a child, or can be used to demonstrate what positive peer interactions can be like for children with behavioral or social difficulties.

Tips for utilizing the strengths perspective when working with children include the following:

- Listen to the child's story.
- Recognize and affirm the child's hurt.
- Search for strengths or good things about the child.
- Find out what the child likes, how he/she has survived in tough times, who helps him/her, when he/she had good times, what he/she is proud of, and his/her aspirations.
- Identify and share the child's strengths or good things with him or her.
- Connect the child's strengths to his or her aspirations.
- Connect the child to people or organizations to help him or her reach his or her chosen aspirations.
- Allow the child to sometimes be in charge when appropriate (Benard, 2002).

By the Lake

By the lake everything seems different, kind of wonderful. I love to go there on Saturday with my mom and dad. We always go for a short hike into the woods and then just sit by the shore. It's so peaceful and serene. I feel all of my troubles just drift away as I feel the breeze touch my face and hear the birds singing happily in the trees.

Sometimes we all talk about happy things, and sometimes we are all quiet. It doesn't really matter, though, because we always have fun. On the way home we often stop for ice cream cones.

By the Lake Activity Sheet: Level 1

Instructions: Write or draw the answers to the following questions.

1. Why does this person like going to the lake?

2. Why does this child like being with his or her parents?

3. What do you like to do with your parents?

4. How would you finish this story?

By the Lake Activity Sheet: Level 2

Instructions: Write or draw the answers to the following questions.

1. What kind of fun things do people you know like to do?

2. Can you tell me about what it is like when they are having fun with friends or family?

3. How does this make them feel?

4. What is their story?

5. How would you change their story if you wanted to?

By the Lake Activity Sheet: Level 3

Instructions: Write or draw the answers to the following questions.

1. What kind of fun things do you like to do?

2. Can you tell me about what it is like when you are having fun with friends or family?

3. How does this make you feel?

4. What is your story?

5. How would you change your story if you wanted to?

My Story: Level 4

Instructions: Write or draw your own story.

It's a Good Thing Activity Sheet 1

Instructions: Write or draw as many good things as you can about the following people, places, and things.

1. Good things about me are

2. Good things about my mom are

3. Good things about my dad are

4. Good things about my _____ are

It's a Good Thing Activity Sheet 2

Instructions: Write or draw as many good things as you can about the following people, places, and things.

1. Good things about my home are

2. Good things about my school are

3. Good things about my neighborhood are

4. Good things about my _____ are

How Do You Have Fun?

Instructions: Write or draw the answers to the following statements.
   Fun with Family:

1. When I am with my dad, we like to

2. When I am with my mom, we like to

3. When I am with my brothers or sisters, we like to

4. When we are all together, we like to

5. When I am with my grandparents, we like to

6. When I am with my cousins, we like to

7. When I am with _____, we like to

Quiz: How Do You Have Fun?

Instructions: Circle the answer or answers that best describe you.
  Fun With Friends Quiz:

1. I have
   a. a lot of friends
   b. a few close friends
   c. no friends

2. When we play, we like to
   a. read books together
   b. play sports together
   c. get in trouble together
   d. do other things together like _____

3. I like friends who are
   a. smart
   b. funny
   c. into sports
   d. really there for me
   e. bad

4. My parents like my friends   True or False

5. My friends like my parents   True or False

6. I am a good friend   True or False

The Great Day

I had the best day ever today. I would say it was a great day! I wore this awesome new pair of jeans to school, and they look really good on me. I wore a new blue hoodie, too. Everybody loved them. They told me I looked great. It made me feel so good.

Then, at the end of the day, we all got our report cards. I got all A's, which rocks. My mom will be so excited when I tell her. Maybe we'll even go out to celebrate!

I can't wait until my soccer team plays tonight. If my luck keeps up, we are sure to win!

The Great Day Activity Sheet: Level 1

Instructions: Write or draw the answers to the following questions.

1. Why is this person having a great day?

2. What does this child like about the day?

3. What do you like about the child's day?

4. How would you finish this story?

The Great Day Activity Sheet: Level 2

Instructions: Write or draw the answers to the following questions.

1. Has anyone you know ever had a great day?

2. Can you tell me about what happened when he or she had a great day?

3. How does this make him or her feel?

4. What is his or her story?

5. How would you change his or her story if you wanted to?

The Great Day Activity Sheet: Level 3

Instructions: Write or draw the answers to the following questions.

1. Have you ever had a great day?

2. Can you tell me about what happened when you had a great day?

3. How does this make you feel?

4. What did you do right to make it a great day?

5. What is your story?

6. How would you change your story if you wanted to?

My Story: Level 4

Instructions: Write or draw your own story.

My Friends

Today after school, my friends Mackenzie and Kamryn came over my house and we had an awesome time. We almost always have a great time when we play together. Today we jumped on my trampoline and then we played hide-and-go-seek. We had so much fun. Mackenzie is really funny and likes to goof off, and Kamryn is a nice person who likes to play sports. I like computers and making videos. We all get along really well, and are all BFFs. We even have BFF bracelets for all three of us.

We all want to get new cell phones so we can text each other all the time. I want a slide phone just like Kamryn's with a texting keyboard. Then we really could text each other a lot. My mom says new phones are expensive. I think I will get one soon, though.

After we played outside, my mom brought us fruit snacks and juice boxes. We ate our snacks while we sat and talked on the trampoline. It was great. We had a really fun day just playing and hanging out at my house.

My Friends Activity Sheet: Level 1

Instructions: Write or draw the answers to the following questions.

1. Why is this child having a fun day?

2. What does this child like about his or her friends?

3. What do you like about the child's day?

4. What did this child do right to make the day fun?

5. How would you finish this story?

My Friends Activity Sheet: Level 2

Instructions: Write or draw the answers to the following questions.

1. Has anyone you know ever had a really fun day?

2. Can you tell me what happened when he or she had a really fun day?

3. How does this make him or her feel?

4. What did he or she do right to make the day fun?

5. What is his or her story?

6. How would you change his or her story if you wanted to?

My Friends Activity Sheet: Level 3

Instructions: Write or draw the answers to the following questions.

1. Have you ever had a really fun day?

2. Can you tell me what happened when you had a really fun day?

3. How does this make you feel?

4. What did you do right to make your day fun?

5. What is your story?

6. How would you change your story if you wanted to?

My Story: Level 4

Instructions: Write or draw your own story.

Strengths Building CHILD Activity

Instructions: Write or draw the answers to the following questions.

Cope ———→   How do you cope when bad things happen?

Hope ———→   What do you hope for?

Identify Inner Strengths ———→ What are your inner strengths?

Love ———→   Who do you love?

Define yourself or Dream ———→ How do you define who you are?

What do you stand for?

What are your dreams?

CHILD Strengths Activity Sheet: Cope

Instructions:

➤ Write or draw a story about: How do I cope when bad things happen in my life?

➤ Then write or draw a story about: What else can I do to cope better in the future when bad things happen in my life?

CHILD Strengths Activity Sheet: Hope

Instructions:

➤ Write or draw a story about: What do I hope for in my life?

CHILD Strengths Activity Sheet: My Hope Plan

Instructions: Make a plan with your counselor, friend, or family member about how to accomplish what you hope to achieve in your life. Include goals in your plan.

I hope that:

My plan is to:

Goals to work toward in my plan include:

1. Goal

2. Goal

3. Goal

CHILD Strengths Activity Sheet:
Identify Inner Strengths

Instructions:

➣ Write or draw a story about your inner strengths. Examples of inner strengths include kindness, having a positive attitude, trying, surviving, intelligence, being a strong person, having a good sense of humor, and other good things. Ask your friends and family to help you find your inner strengths.

CHILD Strengths Activity Sheet: Love

Instructions:

➤ Write or draw a story about: What is love? Give examples about how people can give or show love to each other.

CHILD Strengths Activity Sheet: Define Yourself

Instructions: Write or draw a story about something that represents you and what you stand for. Examples include a peace sign, a smiley face, an animal, a soccer ball, or similar things.

CHILD Strengths Activity Sheet:
Define Yourself Questions

Instructions: Write or draw the answers to the following questions.

What does the character in the story believe in?

What does the character stand for?

What is a symbol that would stand for the character?

What do you believe in?

What do you stand for?

What is a symbol that you would pick to stand for you? (e.g., a smiley face, a peace sign, a tree, an animal, a car, or other symbol)

CHILD Strengths Activity Sheet: Dream

Instructions:

➤ Write or draw a story about: What do I dream about doing or accomplishing in my life? What do I need to do to reach my dreams? Make a plan about how to reach your dreams.

16

Accidents and Injuries

Key Practice Issues and Story Selection

Accidents and injuries occur often in the school-aged population. These can be minor, such as a skinned knee from falling off of one's bike, or catastrophic resulting in death. Unfortunately, accidental injuries may result in serious injuries, such as head injuries, paralysis, or blindness. Also, injuries are the main cause of death of children (Yale Medical Group, 2005). When these accidents happen to a close friend or family member, it can be difficult for children and adults to comprehend. The trauma and ensuing period of adjustment that result after the accident or injury can take time to recover from and work through with caring support.

Many accidents and injuries occur when least expected. Nearly half (45%) of all injuries that result in death actually happen either in the home or nearby. These accidents can include drowning, being shot, being burned, exposure to poison, and falling (Yale Medical Group, 2005). Children may benefit from telling or drawing their traumatic story in a protective, nurturing setting with encouragement to express and articulate their feelings.

Children may also blame themselves for the accident or injury, even though they are not to blame and may not have even been present when the accident occurred. In this situation, it is necessary for the helping professional to deflect blame away from the child. Simple statements from the mental health professional telling the child that it is not his or her fault can aid in alleviating the child's feelings of guilt.

In some situations, the child may have been actively involved in the accident. He or she may have been behaving recklessly or disobeying rules. In this case, it is important for the child to work toward forgiveness of self, and to work toward positive decision-making skills with the therapist. Role-plays may be useful in teaching these decision-making skills.

Symptoms of posttraumatic stress reactions have been found to occur in more than half of children who have experienced some type of traumatic injury, such as in a car accident, fall, or sports injury. Traumatic injury has also been connected to the child experiencing depression and anxiety. In addition, it can be a stressor for the entire family (Kenardy, Thompson, Le Brocque, & Olsson, 2008).

Some symptoms that children may experience after a traumatic injury include:

➤ Avoiding people, places, and activities that remind them of the accident

➤ Becoming upset when they see reminders of events (e.g., nervousness upon viewing automobile accidents on television)

➤ Anxiety when separated from parents (e.g., school refusal)

➤ Recalling the traumatic event repeatedly in one's mind

➤ Trouble sleeping

➤ Acting-out behaviors (Street & Sibert, 1998)

In the story "The Accident," a young child accidentally shoots a friend in the stomach with a pellet gun. Accidental shootings in the United States are not uncommon and continue to injure or kill numerous children and adolescents each year. This story could be used in practice with children who may be behaving irresponsibly or who have accidentally injured someone or been injured themselves.

In "Seeing My Friend in a Wheelchair," a young girl is accidentally hit by a car and is severely injured. This is very traumatic for her friend, who witnessed the event and blames herself for the accident. This would be useful in practice situations where accidents have happened and children are experiencing unjustifiable guilt or blame. It also could be used with children who have been seriously injured.

The Accident

I shot Emily. I didn't mean to shoot her. We were all just playing around in the backyard, and now Emily's in the hospital. You see, I have a pellet gun that I'm allowed to target shoot with. I'm a pretty good shot, or at least I thought I was.

I feel so bad. I really didn't mean to do it. I know I'm not supposed to point it at anyone, but I was just horsing around. I accidentally shot her right in the stomach. They think she's going to be OK. I sure hope so.

It was so scary after it happened, sort of like a bad dream. I ran into the house to tell Mom what had happened. She did not believe me at first, but then she called 911. The ambulance got here really fast. It pulled into my driveway with its lights and siren on. They took poor Emily away in the ambulance. Then my parents had to call Emily's parents. Her mother started to cry when she found out that Emily had been shot.

That evening, my parents threw away my pellet gun, and I am glad they did.

The Accident Activity Sheet: Level 1

Instructions: Draw or write the answers to the following questions.

1. What happened in this story?

2. How does the child telling this story feel?

3. How does the child who was shot with the pellet gun feel?

4. How did this story make you feel?

5. Could this accident have been prevented?

6. How would you finish this story?

The Accident Activity Sheet: Level 2

Instructions: Write or draw the answers to the following questions.

1. Has anyone you know ever been involved in an accidental shooting or other kind of bad accident?

2. Can you tell me what happened when he or she was involved in the accident?

3. How does this make him or her feel?

4. What did he or she do to cope with the accident in a good way?

5. What is his or her story?

6. How would you change his or her story if you could?

The Accident Activity Sheet: Level 3

Instructions: Write or draw the answers to the following questions.

1. Have you ever been involved in an accidental shooting or other kind of bad accident?

2. Can you tell me what happened when you were involved in the accident?

3. How does this make you feel?

4. What did you do to cope with the accident in a good way?

5. What is your story?

6. How would you change your story if you could?

My Story: Level 4

Instructions: Write or draw your own story.

Seeing My Friend in a Wheelchair

by Ashley Slivinske

It was a cold, rainy, and foggy night, so I didn't go with my friend Amber when she went out to get the mail. I assumed that no harm could be done to her, but something did happen. When Amber went out to get the mail, the saddest thing happened. She went out in the road and she got hit by a car. She had even checked to make sure no car was coming.

I ran inside to tell her mom so she could call an ambulance, and she did, but I still did not know if Amber would be OK.

She was in the hospital and the news came. It was so depressing. She had to be in a wheelchair for the rest of her life! I felt like it was all my fault. I ran home to tell my dad.

I should have gone to the mailbox with her. I felt like I hurt Amber, so to deal with it, I hit myself, screamed at myself, and went to my room.

My dad hollered, "Emily, Emily, come down from your room . . . it's not your fault."

"No, it is my fault," I hollered back.

Seeing My Friend in a Wheelchair Activity Sheet: Level 1

Instructions: Write or draw the answers to the following questions.

1. Whose fault was it that Amber got hit by the car?

2. How is Emily feeling?

3. How might Amber be feeling?

4. How does this story make you feel? Why?

5. What could the girls do to cope with what has happened in a positive way?

6. How would you finish this story?

Seeing My Friend in a Wheelchair Activity Sheet: Level 2

Instructions: Write or draw the answers to the following questions.

1. Has anyone you know ever been involved in a bad accident?

2. Can you tell me what happened when he or she was involved in the accident?

3. How does this make him or her feel?

4. What did he or she do to cope with the accident in a good way?

5. What is his or her story?

6. How would you change his or her story if you could?

Seeing My Friend in a Wheelchair Activity Sheet: Level 3

Instructions: Write or draw the answers to the following questions.

1. Have you ever been involved in a bad accident?

2. Can you tell me what happened when you were involved in the bad accident?

3. How does this make you feel?

4. What did you do to cope with the accident in a good way?

5. What is your story?

6. How would you change your story if you could?

My Story: Level 4

Instructions: Write or draw your own story.

How Can I Stay Safe?

Instructions: Write or draw the answers to the following questions.

Saying no to things and people that are bad for you can help you to stay safe.

1. What are some things that you can choose to say no to to help you stay safe?

Saying yes to things and people that are good for you can help you to stay safe.

2. What are some things you can say yes to to help you stay safe?

How Can I Stay Safe? (Possible Answer Sheet)

Instructions: Write or draw the answers to the following questions.

Saying no to things and people that are bad for you can help you to stay safe.

1. What are some things that you can choose to say no to to help you stay safe?

drugs, alcohol, guns, risky behavior, gangs, low self-esteem

Saying yes to things and people that are good for you can help you to stay safe.

2. What are some things you can say yes to to help you stay safe?

seat belts, good friends, sports, academics, helpful parents, common sense, high self-esteem

17

Job Loss and Poverty

Key Practice Issues and Story Selection

Unemployment and poverty impact numerous children and families in the United States today. When parents in the family system are unemployed or employed but earning low wages, it is sometimes difficult for families to meet the very basic needs of their children. Necessities like food, clothing, soap, and laundry detergent can be difficult to acquire when families are struggling financially. This affects everyone in the family, including the children.

Poverty during childhood influences every facet of their lives. It interacts with other life events and contributes to problems such as lack of food, illness and disability, learning issues, lack of housing, and abuse. Families who are poor or unemployed also are more likely to experience increased stress (Noel & Whyte, 2009). Professionals working with children should be aware of formal and informal resources available in their own communities for food, shelter, and employment. Appropriate referrals in their locale should be made and followed up on when necessary (Miley, O'Melia, & DuBois, 2004).

Children raised in a poor community may encounter several adversities, including ". . . lack of physical safety, poor nutrition, lack of early physical exposure to healthy leisure activities, and extensive exposure to violence" (Helton & Smith, 2004, p. 7). These risk factors, though perhaps impossible to completely eliminate in children's lives, may be surmounted by assessing and building on strengths and assets of children, families, and communities. Resiliency in children is more likely to occur when children are supported and loved. Adults concerned about children truly do make a difference in their lives, and can contribute to their ability to triumph over adversity (Helton & Smith).

At times, children may feel overly burdened or worried by additional household or financial responsibilities that may be age inappropriate. Older children may attempt to earn money for the family, while others may be responsible for parenting younger siblings. This may make the child prematurely function as an adult. Embarrassment may also occur when families are proud but in need of assistance. Children in middle childhood often compare themselves to others and will notice differences in style of dress and types of toys, video games, or cell phones owned. Coping can be difficult for all family members.

The story "My Father Lost His Job" was included because it addresses the issues of a family struggling financially and the impact this is having on a child. The child is feeling upset, worried, and burdened by not having enough food in the house. This story could be helpful to children whose families are experiencing financial problems to comfort them in knowing they are not alone.

Numerous strengths may be elicited when discussing the story "We Don't Have a Lot." Although the family is struggling financially, the mother is hardworking, caring, and supportive of her family. She is striving to do her best, and her child recognizes and respects her for this. He also tries to help the family by caring for a younger sibling, which can be positive when done with limits in an age-appropriate manner. Additionally, he has a positive attitude and is considering entering college when he is older. This story could be used to help children and families identify their own strengths, even during challenging times. Also, issues of an absent father may arise and need to be addressed for some children.

My Father Lost His Job

Hi, my name is Chu-Lin. My family received some bad news about 4 months ago—my father lost his job. It has been a struggle ever since. We try to make our money stretch, but it is hard. My father has been looking and looking for work, but he just cannot find a job. It is like there are no jobs out there.

We are barely making it. My mom works part time, and her money is used to pay our rent. We don't have much left over for clothes and food, so we had to start going to the food pantry here in town. They are really nice to us there and give us fresh fruit and meat. My family is very grateful, but I can tell my dad is sometimes embarrassed. We need the help, though . . .

I just wish he could find a good job so we all don't have to worry so much.

My Father Lost His Job Activity Sheet: Level 1

Instructions: Write or draw the answers to the following questions.

1. What is Chu-Lin worried about?

2. How does Chu-Lin feel?

3. How would you feel if you were Chu-Lin?

4. How would you finish this story?

My Father Lost His Job Activity Sheet: Level 2

Instructions: Write or draw the answers to the following questions.

1. Has anyone you know ever lost a job and needed extra help?

2. Can you tell me what happened when he or she lost the job?

3. How did this make him or her feel?

4. What did he or she do to cope with the job loss in a good way?

5. What is his or her story?

6. How would you change his or her story if you could?

My Father Lost His Job Activity Sheet: Level 3

Instructions: Write or draw the answers to the following questions.

1. Has anyone in your family ever lost a job and needed extra help?

2. Can you tell me what happened to you and your family when he or she lost the job?

3. How did this make you feel?

4. How did you and your family cope with the job loss in a good way?

5. What is your story?

6. How would you change your story if you could?

My Story: Level 4

Instructions: Write or draw your own story.

We Don't Have a Lot

My family doesn't have a lot, but that's OK—nobody in my neighborhood does. It is kind of tough where we live. We all just try to get by, and sometimes we help each other out. When my cousin outgrows his clothes, my aunt gives them to my mom and then I get to wear them. I don't really mind. I think his clothes are kind of cool. Then when I am done with them, my little brother wears them.

Once in a while I get to pick out new things, though, which is kind of exciting. Sometimes my mom works an extra shift and makes more money. She's so responsible and works so hard for us. She picks up extra jobs on the side all of the time. I help out by watching my little brother for her. She's a great mom and she really cares about us. I haven't seen my dad in a long time, but I really would like to.

My mom says that when I grow up I am going to college because she couldn't. She thinks education is important. I don't know, maybe she's right.

We Don't Have a Lot Activity Sheet: Level 1

Instructions: Write or draw the answers to the following questions.

1. What is this child's life like?

2. How would you feel if you were this child?

3. What are some good things that are happening in this child's life?

4. Do you think this child will ever go to college?

5. How would you finish this story?

We Don't Have a Lot Activity Sheet: Level 2

Instructions: Write or draw the answers to the following questions.

1. Has anyone you know grown up without having a lot of things?

2. Can you tell me what it was like for him or her not being able to buy a lot of things and not having much money?

3. How does this make him or her feel?

4. What are some good things in this person's life?

5. What is his or her story?

6. How would you finish this person's story?

We Don't Have a Lot Activity Sheet: Level 3

Instructions: Write or draw the answers to the following questions.

1. Have you ever had to go without having some of the things that you wanted or needed?

2. Can you tell me what it was like for you not being able to buy a lot of things and not having much money?

3. How does this make you and your family feel?

4. What are some good things in your life?

5. What is your story?

6. How would you change your story if you could?

My Story: Level 4

Instructions: Write or draw your own story.

18

Military Issues and International Violence

Key Practice Issues and Story Selection

The deployment of parents and other family members can be stressful, frightening, and confusing for children. They also may have conflicting feelings of being proud of the family member, yet upset and frightened about whether the person will return safely. Children whose parents are deployed also are likely to feel increased sadness and experience behavioral problems (DeRanieri, Clements, Clark, Kuhn, & Manno, 2004).

In addition, the child may have difficulty adapting to the new situation of having a parent or family member absent. Adjusting to lost income may pose serious problems for the family as well. There may be additional chores to be done in the family and perhaps less time for the present parent to devote to child care, schoolwork, and play. All of this can be stressful for children who are trying to focus on typical developmental tasks such as schoolwork, friendships, and extracurricular activities.

International violence and terrorism also have an impact on children, either directly or indirectly. Some families and children have lost family members in terrorism attacks. Others have family members who are permanently disabled or ill as a direct result of an attack or from helping after an attack. Even when not directly affected by terrorism, children are still exposed to events related to the threat of terrorism in the media, which are difficult to avoid. Direct and indirect exposure to terrorism can contribute to behavioral problems in children, including sleeping problems and aggression (Wang et al., 2006). Children may also feel unsafe and worried, and exhibit signs of posttraumatic stress (DeRanieri et al., 2004).

In the story "My Dad," the child is concerned about his father's deployment to a war zone very far from home. He worries about his safe return and does not like having him gone. He also is dealing with the family's extra household responsibilities in the absence of the deployed parent. This story will enable the child to identify and acknowledge the emotional challenges faced by children whose parents are in the military.

In the story "It's Scary Out There," a child and his or her family are anxious about traveling in an airplane because of potential terrorist attacks. The family even changes their plans because of concerns over attacks. Unfortunately, fears surrounding terrorism have become a part of everyday reality for children and families today. Mental health professionals can comfort children who have been victims of terrorism and discuss concerns and emotional issues with those who fear its occurrence.

Suggestions for helping the child and family facing military issues include the following:

➤ Emphasize that it is OK to share worries and concerns with family and helping professionals.

➤ Try to maintain a stable family structure even though family dynamics have changed.

➤ When discussing information about war, try to make it developmentally appropriate to meet the needs of the child.

➤ Try to be honest about the situation, and do not make promises to the child that cannot be upheld.

➤ Find ways for the deployed parent and the child to continue an open line of communication via phone, texting, videos, journaling, email, video mail, or instant messaging and so forth (American Academy of Child & Adolescent Psychiatry, 2009).

My Dad

Hi, my name is Devon. I don't understand why Dad had to leave. He has been away before, but this time is different. He is in a war on the other side of the world. I miss him so much, and I am really afraid. I don't want anything bad to happen to him.

I just want him to come home, and so does my mom. We have all been working extra hard while he is away. We have so many extra chores now. Mom even has to cut the grass. Sometimes she cries while she watches the news. I just want everything to go back to normal.

My Dad Activity Sheet: Level 1

Instructions: Write or draw the answers to the following questions.

1. What is Devon worried about?

2. How does Devon feel?

3. How would you feel if you were Devon?

4. What could Devon and his family do to cope better with their situation?

5. How would you finish this story?

My Dad Activity Sheet: Level 2

Instructions: Write or draw the answers to the following questions.

1. Is anyone you know in the military? Has he or she ever had to go away for a long time?

2. Can you tell me what it was like when he or she had to go away for a long time?

3. How did this make him or her feel?

4. What did he or she do to cope with being away?

5. What is his or her story?

6. How would you change his or her story if you could?

My Dad Activity Sheet: Level 3

Instructions: Write or draw the answers to the following questions.

1. Is anyone in your family in the military? Has he or she ever had to go away for a long time?

2. Can you tell me what it was like when he or she had to go away for a long time?

3. How did this make you and your family feel?

4. What did you do to cope with your family member being away?

5. What is your story?

6. How would you change your story if you could?

My Story: Level 4

Instructions: Write or draw your own story.

My Family Member in the Military

Instructions: In the flag, draw a picture or write about the things you miss about your family member.

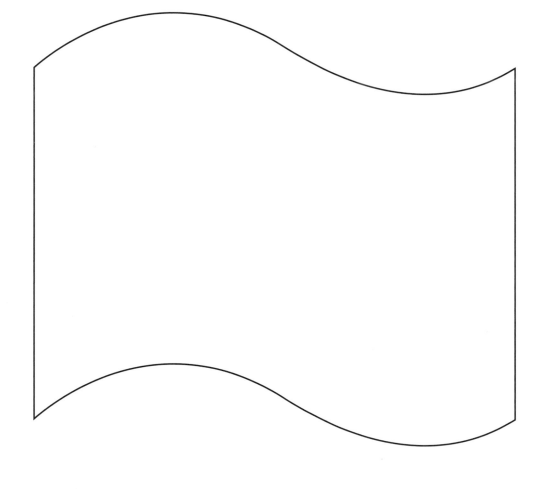

My Family Member in the Military: Letter, Text, or Email

Instructions: Write a letter, text, or email to your family member in the military.

Dear _____:

It's Scary Out There

Sometimes when I watch the news, I become afraid. It's scary out there. People want to blow us up when we fly. We were supposed to fly to Florida this summer to visit the amusement parks, but instead we decided to drive all the way from New York. It will take a very long time, but we don't mind. We are afraid of the terrorists.

I don't understand why they would want to hurt us. We never did anything to them. I wish they would just leave us alone. Then we would not have to worry about being attacked.

It's Scary Out There Activity Sheet: Level 1

Instructions: Write or draw the answers to the following questions.

1. Why is this child afraid?

2. How does this child feel?

3. How would you feel if you were this child?

4. How would you finish this story?

It's Scary Out There Activity Sheet: Level 2

Instructions: Write or draw the answers to the following questions.

1. Has anyone you know ever been afraid of terrorism?

2. Can you tell me what he or she is afraid of?

3. How does this make him or her feel?

4. What could he or she do to feel better?

5. What is his or her story?

6. How would you change his or her story if you could?

It's Scary Out There Activity Sheet: Level 3

Instructions: Write or draw the answers to the following questions.

1. Have you or your family ever been afraid of terrorism?

2. Can you tell me what you are afraid of?

3. How does this make you feel?

4. What could you do to feel better?

5. What is your story?

6. How would you change your story if you could?

My Story: Level 4

Instructions: Write or draw your own story.

19
Death

Key Practice Issues and Story Selection

Unfortunately, death and dying affects our youngest and most vulnerable population. Although children can be resilient, death and the emotions of grieving still affect the development of children in profound ways. Children tend to grieve in the same manner as adults, though their grief reactions are dependent on developmental variations of the child, the type of relationship to the person who has died, and the issues surrounding the death (Stuber & Mesrkhani, 2001).

In 1969, Elisabeth Kübler-Ross wrote *On Death and Dying*, which describes the emotional and psychological experiences of people who are terminally ill. The death of close family and friends also may result in a wide range of emotional and psychological experiences (Kovacs, 2008). There is no right or wrong way to grieve. Also, individuals experience grief in unique ways.

The stages that Kübler-Ross has outlined are similar to the issues children may be facing when adjusting to the death of family members or friends. The stages developed by Kübler-Ross (1969) are adapted to fit the experiences children may face when coping with death and the dying process. Bear in mind variances in the developmental levels of individual children and consider these when applying the following stages of childhood adjustment to death:

➤ *Denial*. The child denies that the person is deceased: "Where is John?" or "Mom is not really dead. She can't be."

➤ *Anger*. The child is angry that he/she is ill or that his/her family member is dead. He/she may act out angry feelings on family and friends: "I hate you!" or "I can't stand you."

➤ *Bargaining*. The child may bargain with others or God in an attempt to change the situation: "God, I won't fight with my little brother anymore if you just bring Dad back."

➤ *Depression*. The child grieves for the loss of a loved one: "I feel sad." He/she may not want to eat or may not want to play.

➤ *Acceptance*. The child accepts his/her life as it is: "I still miss my mom and I always will, but I know she would want me to be happy and play with my friends."

Practical suggestions for helping grieving children include the following:

➤ Listen in a caring, attentive manner to the child's feelings.

➤ Allow the child to openly express his or her deep feelings of sadness.

➤ Assist the child in understanding abstract concepts (afterlife, heaven) based on the family's belief system.

➤ Assist the family and child in deciding whether to attend a funeral of a loved one (Thompson & Rudolph, 1992).

The stories chosen for this book were selected because they cover basic issues surrounding death and children. The story "Scooter" deals with the death of a pet, which many children will experience. This may be the first experience of death that many children will have. It can serve as an opportunity to discuss what death is and what it means to younger children.

"Heaven" is a story about the death of a grandparent, which many children will experience as well. Some children are very close with their grandparents and may rely on them for child care and emotional support. Others may have grandparents as primary caregivers. The story can be used therapeutically to explore basic emotions of grief, belief in an afterlife, and feelings of missing a loved one.

"My Friend's Funeral" discusses the sudden death of a same-aged peer. It addresses the feelings of disbelief and shock that occur when there is a sudden death, especially the death of a child. It also mentions the ambivalent feelings children may have about attending a funeral. The therapist can assist the family in decision making regarding funeral attendance.

"I Can't Believe It" addresses the initial shock and disbelief a child is feeling after the death of her mother, even though her mother suffered with a prolonged illness. In this type of instance, it is not uncommon for people to begin the grieving process while the ill person is still alive, as he or she experiences losses in functioning. Thus, children and family members may experience anticipatory grief, or mourning for losses prior to the actual death of a loved one. The child also is very concerned about what will happen to her and how she will survive without her parent. Realistic caregiving options as well as emotional concerns can be examined with the therapist.

Scooter

Hi, I'm Chen. I have a dog named Scooter. Well, at least I did. He got really sick and we took him to the veterinarian. My dad said they tried to help him. I guess the vet could not make him better.

I found out yesterday that Scooter died. I started crying when I found out. My dad even cried. I've never seen him cry before. We all loved Scooter very much.

Scooter Activity Sheet: Level 1

Instructions: Write or draw the answers to the following questions.

1. How do Chen and his dad feel?

2. What happened to Scooter?

3. What could they do to feel better?

4. How would you finish this story?

Scooter Activity Sheet: Level 2

Instructions: Write or draw the answers to the following questions.

1. Has anyone you know ever had a pet die?

2. Can you tell me what happened when the pet died?

3. How did this make him or her feel?

4. What did he or she do to feel better after the pet died?

5. What is his or her story?

6. How would you change his or her story if you could?

Scooter Activity Sheet: Level 3

Instructions: Write or draw the answers to the following questions.

1. Have you ever had a pet die?

2. Can you tell me what happened when the pet died?

3. How did this make you feel?

4. What did you do to feel better after the pet died?

5. What is your story?

6. How would you change your story if you could?

My Story: Level 4

Instructions: Write or draw your own story.

Heaven

I miss my grandma. She was a nice lady. I used to go to her house every Saturday, and she would watch me while Mom worked.

Then Grandma had to go to the hospital because she felt really sick. They told me she was going to get better, but she didn't. They say that Grandma is in heaven. Heaven is where people go when they die.

I just wish Grandma would come back from heaven so she could play with me again. Mom misses her, too. Sometimes she starts to cry when she talks about her.

Heaven Activity Sheet: Level 1

Instructions: Write or draw the answers to the following questions.

1. What happened to this child's grandma?

2. How is this child feeling?

3. How can this child cope with the death of her grandma?

4. Have you ever felt like the child in the story?

5. How would you finish this story?

Heaven Activity Sheet: Level 2

Instructions: Write or draw the answers to the following questions.

1. Has anyone you know ever had a friend or family member die?

2. Can you tell me about what happened when he or she had a friend or family member die?

3. How does this make him or her feel?

4. What did he or she do to cope with the death in a good way?

5. What is his or her story?

6. How would you change his or her story if you could?

Heaven Activity Sheet: Level 3

Instructions: Write or draw the answers to the following questions.

1. Have you ever had a friend or family member die?

2. Can you tell me about what happened when your friend or family member died?

3. How does this make you feel?

4. What did you do to cope with the death in a good way?

5. What is your story?

6. How would you change your story if you could?

My Story: Level 4

Instructions: Write or draw your own story.

My Friend's Funeral

Hi, my name is Josh. I just got some really bad news. My friend Bailey died. He was riding his bike on our road and he got hit by a car. I just can't believe it. I don't believe it. He can't be dead. We just played baseball together yesterday, and tomorrow is our scout meeting.

How can a kid die?

My parents say that we will go to calling hours and his funeral in a few days. I've never been to a funeral. I am kind of scared. I don't really want to go.

My Friend's Funeral Activity Sheet: Level 1

Instructions: Write or draw the answers to the following questions.

1. What happened to Josh's friend Bailey?

2. How is Josh feeling?

3. Have you ever felt like Josh?

4. What could Josh do to cope with his feelings?

5. How would you finish this story?

My Friend's Funeral Activity Sheet: Level 2

Instructions: Write or draw the answers to the following questions.

1. Has anyone you know ever had a friend die?

2. Can you tell me about what happened when he or she had a friend die?

3. How does this make him or her feel?

4. What did he or she do to cope with the death of a friend?

5. What is his or her story?

6. How would you change his or her story if you could?

My Friend's Funeral Activity Sheet: Level 3

Instructions: Write or draw the answers to the following questions.

1. Have you ever had a friend die?

2. Can you tell me about what happened when your friend died?

3. How does this make you feel?

4. What can you do to cope with your friend's death?

5. What is your story?

6. How would you change your story if you could?

My Story: Level 4

Instructions: Write or draw your own story.

I Can't Believe It

"I just can't believe it," Latika thought to herself. "My mother is dead. It just can't be! What is going to happen to me without her? I just want her back!"

Latika's mother had been sick for a very, very long time—almost from the time she could remember. Her mother used to have to go to the hospital a lot, and Latika's aunts would take turns watching her when her mother was sick. It was very hard for Latika seeing her mother getting sicker and sicker. She just wanted to make her better—but she couldn't. Not even the doctors could make her better, or God.

"I just don't know what I am going to do now. What will my life be like without my mother?"

I Can't Believe It Activity Sheet: Level 1

Instructions: Write or draw **the answers** to the following questions.

1. What happened to Latika's mother?

2. How is Latika feeling?

3. Have you ever felt the way that Latika feels?

4. What could Latika do to cope with the death of her mother?

5. How would you finish this story?

I Can't Believe It Activity Sheet: Level 2

Instructions: Write or draw the answers to the following questions.

1. Has anyone you know ever had a parent die?

2. Can you tell me about what happened when his or her parent died?

3. How does this make him or her feel?

4. How did he or she cope with the death of his or her parent?

5. What is his or her story?

6. How would you change his or her story if you could?

I Can't Believe It Activity Sheet: Level 3

Instructions: Write or draw the answers to the following questions.

1. Have you ever had a parent die?

2. Can you tell me about what happened when your mom or dad died?

3. How does this make you feel?

4. How are you coping with the death of your parent?

5. What is your story?

6. How would you change your story if you could?

My Story: Level 4

Instructions: Write or draw your own story.

Coping Skills Activity Sheet

Write or draw five things that can help you to cope positively with the death of your loved one.

Write or draw five things that are not helping you to cope with the death of your loved one.

20

General Activity Sheets for All Practice Areas

The following activity sheets may be used with multiple practice areas. Please adapt, modify, or customize them if necessary to meet the individualized needs of clients.

General Story Activities

1. **Role-Plays**: Take the role of any character in the story. Have your therapist, family, or other children take the roles of other characters. Act out the story in your assigned roles.

2. **Songs**: Make up a song about the story or the situation in your life. Sing it to your therapist, or perform it for your family if you want to. Add dance moves if you like.

3. **Games**: Make up a board game or an active game about the story or the situation in your life. Running, jumping, and bouncing are allowed, with permission from your therapist. Play the game with your therapist, family, or friends.

4. **Collages**: Make a collage about your story. Cut out pictures from old magazines, use photos you have taken, or print pictures from the Internet. Paste them onto a poster board to describe the story.

All About Me Story

Instructions: Write or draw your own story about you.

My Story

Instructions: Write or draw your own story.

My Perfect Day

Instructions: Write or draw a story about your perfect day.

Lifemap

Instructions: Map the story of your life using the circles and arrows shown below. Use pictures and words to tell the story of your life from when you were born until now.

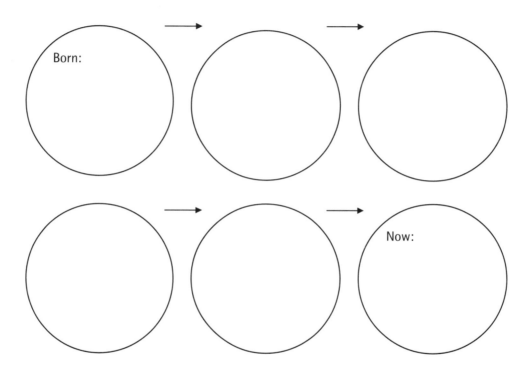

General Story Activity Sheet

Instructions: Write or draw the answers to the following questions.

1. Has anything like this ever happened to you or to anyone you know?

2. What is this person's story? What happened in this person's life?

3. How does this make you feel?

4. How does this person cope with what happened?

5. How would you finish this person's story?

My Letter

Instructions: Write a letter to _____. You do not need to send the letter.

Dear _____:

Parent's Letter to Child

Instructions: Write a letter to _____. You do not need to send the letter.

Dear _____:

Therapist's Letter to a Child

Dear _____, this is what I hope and dream for you.

Text or Email Activity Sheet

Text or email your family member or friend. You do not need to send the text or email.

Dear _____:

Therapist's Letter to a Child

Dear _____, this is what I like about you.

Texting Story Page

Instructions: Text your own story.

    For example, use the following types of texting phrases to tell your story: omg (oh my god), bff (best friend forever), thx (thanks), brb (be right back), ttyl (talk to you later), gr8 (great), gtg (got to go), 4evr (forever), fyeo (for your eyes only), jp (just playing), hr8 (heart), b4n (bye for now), etc.

Family Homes Activity Sheet

Instructions: Draw a picture of your home (or homes). List five things that you like and dislike about your home (or homes).

Coping Skills Activity Sheet

Write or draw five things that can help you to cope positively.

Write or draw five things that are not helping you to cope.

It's a Good Thing Activity Sheet 1

Instructions: Write or draw as many good things as you can about the following people, places, and things.

1. Good things about me are

2. Good things about my mom are

3. Good things about my dad are

4. Good things about my _____ are

It's a Good Thing Activity Sheet 2

Instructions: Write or draw as many good things as you can about the following people, places, and things.

1. Good things about my home are

2. Good things about my school are

3. Good things about my neighborhood are

4. Good things about my _____ are

How Do You Have Fun?

Instructions: Write or draw the answers to the following statements.
Fun With Family:

1. When I am with my dad, we like to

2. When I am with my mom, we like to

3. When I am with my brothers or sisters, we like to

4. When we are all together, we like to

5. When I am with my grandparents, we like to

6. When I am with my cousins, we like to

7. When I am with _____, we like to

Quiz: How Do You Have Fun?

Instructions: Circle the answer or answers that best describe you.
Fun with Friends Quiz:

1. I have
   a. a lot of friends
   b. a few close friends
   c. no friends

2. When we play we like to
   a. read books together
   b. play sports together
   c. get in trouble together
   d. do other things together like _____

3. I like friends who are
   a. smart
   b. funny
   c. into sports
   d. really there for me
   e. bad

4. My parents like my friends   True or False

5. My friends like my parents   True or False

6. I am a good friend   True or False

Strengths Building CHILD Activity

Instructions: Write or draw the answers to the following questions.

Cope ⟶   How do you cope when bad things happen?

Hope ⟶   What do you hope for?

Identify Inner Strengths ⟶   What are your inner strengths?

Love ⟶   Who do you love?

Define yourself or Dream ⟶   How do you define who you are?

What do you stand for?

What are your dreams?

CHILD Strengths Activity Sheet: Cope

Instructions:

➢ Write or draw a story about: How do I cope when bad things happen in my life?

➢ Then write or draw a story about: What else can I do to cope better in the future when bad things happen in my life?

CHILD Strengths Activity Sheet: Hope

Instructions:

➤ Write or draw a story about: What do I hope for in my life?

CHILD Strengths Activity Sheet: My Hope Plan

Instructions: Make a plan with your counselor, friend, or family member about how to accomplish what you hope to achieve in your life. Include goals in your plan.

I hope that:

My plan is to:

Goals to work toward my plan include:

1. Goal

2. Goal

3. Goal

CHILD Strengths Activity Sheet:
Identify Inner Strengths

Instructions: Write or draw a story about your inner strengths. Examples of inner strengths include kindness, having a positive attitude, trying, surviving, intelligence, being a strong person, having a good sense of humor, and other good things. Ask your friends and family to help you find your inner strengths.

CHILD Strengths Activity Sheet: Love

Instructions:

➤ Write or draw a story about: What is love? Give examples about how people can give or show love to each other.

CHILD Strengths Activity Sheet: Define Yourself

Instructions: Write or draw a story about something that represents you and what you stand for. Examples include a peace sign, a smiley face, an animal, a soccer ball, or similar things.

CHILD Strengths Activity Sheet: Define Yourself Questions

Instructions: Write or draw the answers to the following questions.

What does the character in the story believe in?

What does the character **stand** for?

What is a symbol that **would stand** for the character?

What do you believe in?

What do you stand for?

What is a symbol that **you would** pick to stand for you? (e.g., a smiley **face, a peace** sign, a tree, an animal, a **car, or other** symbol)

CHILD Strengths Activity Sheet: Dream

Instructions:

➢ Write or draw a story about: What do I dream about doing or accomplishing in my life? What do I need to do to reach my dreams? Make a plan about how to reach your dreams.

Create a Game Activity Sheet

Instructions: In the space provided or on your own, create a game about _____.
Play it with your therapist, family, or other kids. Create game pieces to use with the
game.

Self-Esteem Booster

Instructions: Write or draw the answers to the following questions.

1. What am I good at doing?

2. What am I not good at doing?

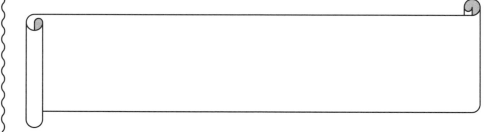

3. What do I want to improve?

Child's Reward Chart

Instructions: Place a check mark, sticker, or star in the box when desired behavior is achieved.

🙂	Monday	Tuesday	Wednesday	Thursday	Friday	Saturday	Sunday
Homework							
Chores							
Good Behavior							

References

American Academy of Child & Adolescent Psychiatry. (2009). *Families in the military*. Retrieved July 11, 2009, from http://aacap.org/page.ww?name=Families+in+the+Military&section=Facts+for+Families.

Angus, L. E., & McLeod, J. (Eds.). (2004). *The handbook of narrative and psychotherapy: Practice, theory, and research*. Thousand Oaks, CA: Sage.

Arman, J. F., & McNair, R. (2000). A small group model for working with elementary school children of alcoholics. *Professional School Counseling, 3*(4), 290–293.

Asher, S. R., & Williams, G. (1993). Children without friends, Part 1: Their problems. In C. M. Todd (Ed.), *Day Care Center Connections, 2*(6), 3–4. Urbana-Champaign, IL: University of Illinois Cooperative Extension Service.

Bandura, A., & Walters, R. H. (1963). *Social learning and personality development*. New York: Holt, Rinehart, & Winston.

Barker, R. L. (1995). *The social work dictionary* (3rd ed.). Washington, DC: NASW Press.

Barker, R. L. (2003). *The social work dictionary* (5th ed.). Washington, DC: NASW Press.

Baumrind, D. (1971). Current patterns of parental authority. *Developmental Psychology Monographs, 4*(1, Pt.2), 1–103.

Benard, B. (2002). Turnaround people and places: Moving from risk to resilience. In D. Saleebey (Ed.), *The strengths perspective in social work practice* (3rd ed., pp. 213–227). Boston: Allyn & Bacon.

Burns, G. W. (2005). *101 Healing stories for kids and teens: Using metaphors in therapy*. Hoboken, NJ: Wiley.

Button, D. M., & Payne, B. K. (2009). Training child protective services workers about domestic violence: Needs, strategies, and barriers. *Children and Youth Services Review, 31*(3), 364–369.

Carlson, J. M. (1999). Cooperative games: A pathway to improving health. *Professional School Counseling, 2,* 230–236.

Carr, A. (2007). *Family therapy: Concepts, process, and practice* (2nd ed.). Hoboken, NJ: Wiley.

Charlesworth, L., Wood, J., & Viggiani, P. (2008). Middle childhood. In E. D. Hutchison (Ed.), *Dimensions of human behavior: The changing life course* (3rd ed., pp. 175–226). Thousand Oaks, CA: Sage.

Child Welfare Information Gateway. (2008). *What is child abuse and neglect?* Retrieved July 4, 2009, from www.childwelfare.gov/pubs/factsheets/whatiscan.cfm.

Clements, P. T., Benasutti, K. M., & Henry, G. C. (2001). Drawing from experience: Utilizing drawings to facilitate communication and understanding with children exposed to sudden traumatic deaths. *Journal of Psychosocial Nursing, 39*(12), 12–20.

Cohen, G. J., & Committee on Psychosocial Aspects of Child and Family Health. (2002). Helping children and families deal with divorce and separation. *Pediatrics, 110*(5), 1019–1023.

Cohen, J. A., Mannarino, A. P., & Deblinger, E. (2006). *Treating trauma and traumatic grief in children and adolescents*. New York: Guilford Press.

Coles, R. (1987). *The moral life of children*. Boston: Houghton Mifflin.

Coles, R. (1997). *The moral intelligence of children*. New York: Random House.

Crenshaw, D. A. (2008). *Therapeutic engagement of children and adolescents: Play, symbol, drawing, and storytelling strategies*. Plymouth, UK: Aronson.

Crosson-Tower, C. (2009). *Exploring child welfare: A practice perspective* (5th ed.). Boston: Pearson Education.

DeLucia-Waack, J. L. (2006). *Leading psychoeducational groups for children and adolescents.* Thousand Oaks, CA: Sage.

DeRanieri, J. T., Clements, P. T., Clark, K., Kuhn, D. W., & Manno, M. S. (2004). War, terrorism, and children. *Journal of School Nursing, 20*(2), 69–75.

Divinyi, J. E. (1995). Storytelling: An enjoyable and effective therapeutic tool. *Contemporary Family Therapy, 17*(1), 27–37.

Frantz, T. G. (1995). Stories for therapy: The right story to the right person at the right time. *Contemporary Family Therapy, 17*(1), 47–64.

Freeman, L., Mokros, H., & Pozanski, E. (1993). Violent events reported by urban school-age children: Characteristics and depression correlates. *Journal of the American Academy of Child and Adolescent Psychiatry, 32,* 419–423.

Gardner, H. (1983). *Frames of mind: The theory of multiple intelligences.* New York: Basic Books.

Gardner, H. (1993). *Multiple intelligences: The theory in practice.* New York: Basic Books.

Gardner, H. (2009). Birth and the spreading of a "meme." In J. Chen, S. Moran, & H. Gardner (Eds.), *Multiple intelligences around the world* (pp. 3–16). San Francisco: Jossey-Bass.

Gardner, P. J., & Poole, J. M. (2009). One story at a time: Narrative therapy, older adults, and addictions. *Journal of Applied Gerontology, 28*(5), 600–620.

Gardner, R. A. (1971). *Therapeutic communication with children: The mutual storytelling technique.* New York: Science House.

Geldard, D. (2009). Promoting self-care behaviours. In K. Geldard (Ed.), *Practical interventions for young people at risk* (pp. 13–21). London: Sage.

Geldard, K., & Geldard, D. (2008). *Counselling children: A practical introduction* (3rd ed.). London: Sage.

Gibbs, J. T., & Huang, L. N., and associates. (2003). *Children of color: Psychological interventions with culturally diverse youth* (2nd ed.). San Francisco: Jossey-Bass.

Glasser, W. (1984). *Control theory: A new explanation of how we control our lives.* New York: Harper & Row.

Glasser, W. (1998). *Choice theory: A new psychology of personal freedom.* New York: Harper Perennial.

Golding, J. (2006). *Healing stories: Picture books for the big & small changes in a child's life.* Lanham, MD: Evans.

Gray, B., & Ridden, G. (1999). *Lifemaps of people with learning disabilities.* London: Kingsley.

Green, M., & Palfrey, J. S. (Eds.). (2001). Bright futures family tip sheets: Middle childhood. *Bright futures.* Arlington, VA: National Center for Education in Maternal and Child Health.

Harris, M. B. (2006). Best school-based practices with adolescent parents. In C. Franklin, M. B. Harris, & P. Allen-Meares (Eds.), *The school services sourcebook: A guide for school-based professionals* (pp. 337–344). New York: Oxford University Press.

Helton, L. R., & Smith, M. K. (2004). *Mental health practice with children and youth: A strengths and well-being model.* Binghamton, NY: Haworth Social Work Practice Press.

Hepworth, D. H., Rooney, R. H., Rooney, G. D., Strom-Gottfried, K., & Larsen, J. (2006). *Direct social work practice* (7th ed.). Belmont, CA: Thomson Brooks/Cole.

Hutchison, E. D. (2008). *Dimensions of human behavior: The changing life course* (3rd ed.). Thousand Oaks, CA: Sage.

Jolley, R. (2010). *Children & pictures: Drawing and understanding.* West Sussex, UK: Wiley-Blackwell.

Josephs, M. (2005). Art, drama, and play therapies. In M. Cooper, C. Hooper, & M. Thompson (Eds.), *Child and adolescent mental health: Theory and practice* (pp. 200–205). London: Hodder Arnold.

Kenardy, J., Thompson, K., Le Brocque, R., & Olsson, K. (2008). Information-provision intervention for children and their parents following pediatric accidental injury. *European Child & Adolescent Psychiatry, 17*(5), 316–324.

Kohlberg, L. (1969). Stage and sequence: The cognitive-developmental approach to socialization. In D. A. Goslin (Ed.), *Handbook of socialization theory and research* (pp. 347–480). Chicago: Rand McNally.

Kohlberg, L. (1976). Moral stages and moralization: The cognitive-developmental approach. In T. Lickona (Ed.), *Moral development and behavior: Theory, research, and social issues* (pp. 31–53). New York: Holt, Rinehart & Winston.

Kovacs, P. J. (2008). Very late adulthood. In E. D. Hutchison (Ed.), *Dimensions of human behavior: The changing life course* (3rd ed., pp. 417–452). Thousand Oaks, CA: Sage.

Kübler-Ross, E. (1969). *On death and dying.* New York: Macmillan.

Lageman, A. G. (1990). The moral lives of children: The thought of Robert Coles. *Journal of Religion and Health, 29*(4), 303–307.

Lambie, G. W., & Sias, S. M. (2005). Children of alcoholics: Implications for professional school counseling. *Professional School Counseling, 8*(3), 266–273.

Lieberman, A. F., & Van Horn, P. (2008). *Psychotherapy with infants and young children: Repairing the effects of stress and trauma on early attachment.* New York: Guilford Press.

Livio, N. J. (1994). *Who's afraid . . .? Facing children's fears with folktales.* Englewood, CO: Teacher Ideas Press.

Medicinenet. (2009). *Child abuse.* Retrieved July 4, 2009, from www.medicinenet.com/child_abuse/article.htm.

Miley, K. K., O'Melia, M., & DuBois, B. (2004). *Generalist social work practice: An empowering approach* (4th ed.). Boston: Allyn & Bacon.

Mize, J., & Abell, E. (2009). *Encouraging social skills in young children: Tips teachers can share with parents.* Retrieved July 16, 2009, from http://humsci.auburn.edu/parent/socialskills.html.

Morgan, A. (2000). *What is narrative therapy? An easy-to-read introduction.* Adelaide, Australia: Dulwich Centre.

National Library of Medicine and the National Institutes of Health. (2009). Medline Plus: *Bullying.* Retrieved June 22, 2009, from www.nlm.nih.gov/medlineplus/bullying.html.

Newman, B. M., & Newman, P. R. (2006). *Development through life: A psychosocial approach* (9th ed.). Belmont, CA: Thomson Wadsworth.

Nichols, M. P. (2008). *Family therapy: Concepts and methods* (8th ed.). Boston: Allyn & Bacon.

Noel, J. A., & Whyte, D. L. (2009). Children and poverty. In C. Crosson-Tower (Ed.), *Exploring child welfare: A practice perspective* (5th ed., pp. 63–86). Boston: Pearson Education.

Robinson, B. E., & Rhoden, J. L. (1998). *Working with children of alcoholics: The practitioner's handbook* (2nd ed.). Thousand Oaks, CA: Sage.

Saleebey, D. (2002). *The strengths perspective in social work practice* (3rd ed.). Boston: Allyn & Bacon.

Schmidt, M. M. (2001). Using play therapy assessment in an elementary and intermediate school setting. In A. A. Drewes, L. J. Carey, & C. E. Schaefer (Eds.), *School-based play therapy* (pp. 3–15). New York: Wiley.

Slattery, J. M. (2004). *Counseling diverse clients: Bringing context into therapy.* Belmont, CA: Brooks/Cole-Thomson Learning.

Slivinske, L. R., & Fitch, V. L. (1987). The effect of control enhancing interventions on the well-being of elderly individuals living in retirement communities. *Gerontologist, 27*(2), 176–181.

Street, E., & Sibert, J. (1998). Post-traumatic stress reactions in children. *Clinical Child Psychology and Psychiatry, 3*(4), 553–560.

Stuber, M. L., & Mesrkhani, V. H. (2001). What do we tell the children? Understanding childhood grief. *Western Journal of Medicine, 174,* 187–191.

Terjesen, M. D., Jacofsky, M., Froh, J., & DiGiuseppe, R. (2004). Integrating positive psychology into schools: Implications for practice. *Psychology in the Schools, 41*(1), 163–172.

Thompson, C. L., & Rudolph, L. B. (1992). *Counseling children* (3rd ed.). Pacific Grove, CA: Brooks/Cole.

U.S. Census Bureau. (2006). *Statistical abstract of the United States* (126th ed.). Washington, DC: Author.

Wallerstein, J. S. (1983). Children of divorce: The psychological tasks of the child. *American Journal of Orthopsychiatry, 53,* 230–243.

Wang, Y., Nomura, Y., Pat-Horenczyk, R., Doppelt, O., Abramovitz, R., Brom, D., et al. (2006). Association of direct exposure to terrorism, media exposure to terrorism, and other trauma with emotional and behavioral problems with preschool children. *Annals of the New York Academy of Sciences, 1094,* 363–368; doi: 10.1196/annals.1376.051

Webb, N. B. (1991). Play therapy crisis intervention with children. In N. B. Webb (Ed.), *Play therapy with children in crisis: A casebook for practitioners* (pp. 26–42). New York: Guilford Press.

Wegscheider, S. (1981). *Another chance: Hope and health for the alcoholic family.* Palo Alto, CA: Science and Behavior Books.

Williams, L. T. (2009). Counseling for families and children. In C. Crosson-Tower (Ed.), *Exploring child welfare: A practice perspective* (5th ed., pp. 148–180). Boston: Pearson Education.

Woody, D. J. (2008). Infancy and toddlerhood. In E. D. Hutchison (Ed.), *Dimensions of human behavior: The changing life course* (3rd ed., pp. 95–135). Thousand Oaks, CA: Sage.

Woody, D. J., & Woody, D. III (2008). Early childhood. In E. D. Hutchison (Ed.), *Dimensions of human behavior: The changing life course* (3rd ed., pp. 137–173). Thousand Oaks, CA: Sage.

Yale Medical Group: The Physicians of Yale University (2005). *Common childhood injuries and poisonings: Accident statistics.* Retrieved July 13, 2009, from www.ymghealthinfo.org/content.asp?pageid=P02853.

Zastrow, C. H., & Kirst-Ashman, K. K. (2010). *Understanding human behavior and the social environment* (8th ed.). Belmont, CA: Brooks/Cole.

Author Index

Abell, E., 97
American Academy of Child &
    Adolescent Psychiatry, 270
Angus, L. E., 12
Arman, J. F., 185
Asher, S. R., 97

Bandura, A., 30
Barker, R. L., 16–17, 28, 213
Baumrind, D., 82
Benard, B., 22, 214
Benasutti, K. M., 15
Burns, G. W., 7
Button, D. M., 133–134

Carlson, J. M., 16
Carr, A., 12
Charlesworth, L., 26, 29, 199
Child Welfare Information
    Gateway, 163
Clark, K., 269–270
Clements, P. T., 15, 269–270
Cohen, G. J., 117
Cohen, J. A., 13
Coles, R., 30
Committee on Psychosocial
    Aspects of Child and Family
    Health, 117
Crenshaw, D. A., 3, 19, 24
Crosson-Tower, C., 117, 145

Deblinger, E., 13
DeLucia-Waack, J. L., 16
DeRanieri, J. T., 269–270
DiGiuseppe, R., 20
Divinyi, J. E., 8–9, 14
Dubois, B., 20–21, 257

Erikson, E., 27–28

Fitch, V. L., 17
Frantz, T. G., 5
Freeman, L., 145
Froh, J., 20

Gardner, H., 25
Gardner, P. J., 12
Gardner, R. A., 7
Geldard, D., 11, 13–14, 17, 97
Geldard, K., 11, 13–14
Gibbs, J. T., 31
Glasser, W., 17
Golding, J., 12–14
Gray, B., 12
Green, M., 27–28

Harris, M. B., 98
Helton, L. R., 12, 15, 19,
    257–258
Henry, G. C., 15
Hepworth, D. H., 20
Huang, L. N., 31
Hutchison, E. D., 81

Jacofsky, M., 20
Jolley, R., 15
Josephs, M., 14, 16–17

Kenardy, J., 244
Kirst-Ashman, K. K., 28–29,
    61–62, 164
Kohlberg, L., 30
Kovacs, P. J., 33, 283
Kübler-Ross, E., 33, 283
Kuhn, D. W., 269–270

Subject Index